The Mentor Group, Inc.
Atlanta, Georgia

RAGS
TO
RICHES
TO
RAGS
TO
RICHES

(Third Edition)

by John Ross, with Steve Osborne

Library of Congress Cataloging in Publication Data

Ross, John.
    Rags to riches to rags to riches.

91-090179
ISBN 1-879868-00-8

Cover design by Rob Simpson

Printed in the United States of America

I'd like to publicly thank my Heavenly Father for all my blessings and for giving me a second chance at life; my friends and family for their support; and my wife, Kelly Kay, for believing in me from the first day we met.

– John Ross

Foreword

When John and I discussed how we were going to end this book, I suggested that we make reference to the song Frank Sinatra made famous: *My Way*. You probably remember bits and pieces of the lyrics, like "... the record shows, I took the blows, and did it my way."

The song seemed appropriate for John's story. But at the time I suggested it, I was only halfway through the book. As I moved toward the conclusion, it became clear that the song wasn't at all right for John. The words seemed too arrogant.

And John is not arrogant. Energetic, yes. Enthusiastic, yes. Confident, yes. But arrogant? No.

He *could* have been. If life had left him alone when he first made it "big" – if he had continued making lots of money without setbacks and challenges – there's a good chance that John would be a shallow, arrogant person today. I say that because that's what often happens to people who live under consistently easy circumstances.

But life has *not* been easy for John. Instead of rolling out an endless red carpet for him, it tripped him, kicked him, slapped him, beat him up, and then pulled the rug out from under him altogether.

What happened to John – as you'll read in this book – was enough to break most people. But John isn't "most people." Every time he got knocked down, he somehow got up again, even if it was only on his knees.

Finally, his determination to get on his feet and stay there made him tough enough and strong enough to take the blows and move ahead toward his goals.

We tend to envy people who have everything and haven't had to struggle to get it. But for those who have had to fight through obstacles and trials before they could grab their brass rings, we reserve something very different than envy – we give them our admiration.

I admire John Ross.

I say that not only because he has jumped incredible hurdles to get where he is, but also because in jumping those hurdles, he has become a better, stronger person than he was before. The crucible of adversity has made him sincere where he could have been arrogant, caring where he could have been self-centered, confident where he could have been cocky.

In John's case, his worst problems have become his greatest blessings. They have made him what he is. That's what's so exciting about his story. It confirms what the great moral teachers have always taught: that obstacles can force us to leap to greater heights; that our weaknesses can indeed become our strengths.

I finally suggested a different way to end the book. We still made reference to the lyrics of a song, but it's a song with a very different feel than *My Way*. It's a song you've undoubtedly heard many times. After reading this book, I think you'll agree that *Amazing Grace* is much more appropriate to John's story.

– Steve Osborne

Table of Contents

"You're Under Arrest!"

The two men that walked into my office could have been Realtors, investors, or Xerox salesmen. They were clean-cut, conservatively dressed. They exuded an air of quiet confidence.

"Are you John Ross?"

"Yes," I answered.

"Mr. Ross, we're with the FBI, and you're under arrest."

There are moments in life when time virtually stands still. This was one of them. I stared in amazement at these men, trying to make sense of what they had just said. The words "under arrest" came to me like a phrase out of an old James Cagney movie. They were make-believe words. They weren't words that you ever hear in real life. Not in *my* life, anyway. Yet here were two men telling me I was under arrest.

All time and motion ground to a halt, and a succession of still-framed memories exploded in my mind in rapid succession. I saw myself sitting in church with my wife and four children – a father proud of his family; a family proud of its father. I saw myself being interviewed on a local *Good Morning America*-type television show – a young man who had achieved uncommon success in real estate investments. I saw myself standing in front of a group of students who thought of me as a master who could help them walk the golden path to success and financial liberation. *This* was reality.

"You must come with us," said one of the agents.

I made a desperate attempt to gather my wits. "If this is real," I thought, "if this isn't a nightmare, what should I do?" I forced my voice to sound calm. "I'd like to call my lawyer," I told them. "Will you please have a seat?"

Minutes later, when I emerged from my office between the two FBI agents (mercifully, they did not handcuff me), I was horrified to see several television news cameras pointing directly at me. These were cameras from the same stations that had been spotlighting my success story during the past years – stations that had labelled me a rising young business star. Now they were here, like buzzards, to video my arrest and pick my bones.

At the police station I was fingerprinted and booked. Mug shots were taken, and I was told that I had been charged with ten counts of grand larceny. Then I was placed in a cell and the heavy, barred door was shut and locked.

I didn't fully realize it at the time, but that simple yet symbolic turning of the key was to separate me forever from the people I loved so dearly and the life I had worked so hard to build. It's fortunate that I didn't fully understand at that time how my arrest would affect my life. I don't think I could have taken it.

"This *can't* be happening," I kept telling myself. "It's just a nightmare. That's all. I'll wake up in my own bed, in my own house, next to my wife, any minute now." My lips formed these words over and over again, like a Hindu mantra. And as they did, my mind – wounded and in a state of shock – began searching through the past.

Looking back, I realize now that I was frantically looking for clues to help me make sense of what was happening. In my 28 years, I had risen higher than most people ever dream of. And now I had fallen lower than I had ever imagined possible. I had been on the very top. And now I was bankrupt and in jail.

"Why is this happening to *me*?" I thought. "Why has my life been such a roller-coaster of fortune? Why?" Out of the timeless scrapbook of memory, my numbed mind began pulling bits and pieces of the past together. Maybe in those shards of remembrance I would find an answer....

The Life of the Party

It was past my bedtime and I was laughing and talking with my mother and her friends. I had school the next morning, and my first-grade teacher always told us we'd be tired if we stayed up past bedtime. But I was never tired. I always had more energy than I knew what to do with. I often got to stay up late when Mom had parties, which she often did. She let me stay up late because I was the life of the party.

My mother was a full-blooded Sicilian. She wasn't a loud, boisterous Sicilian – like the stereotype you see in the movies. But she had strong passions, a zest for life, and she loved people.

She used to throw a lot of parties and I was often a part of them. Even when I was two and three years old and had gone to sleep early, my mom's friends would come over to parties at our house, and they'd say, "Wake the kid up," and I'd come down and entertain them. I can't remember exactly what I did. But I think I just stood there in front of them and talked. Whatever it was I did, they liked it enough to wake me up when they came over.

My mother's parties weren't black tie affairs. They were casual house parties. She'd sometimes have 50, 60, or even 70 people over. The women would be upstairs talking. The men would be downstairs watching football or playing pool. I wasn't much interested in watching sports because I played them all the time, so I usually stayed upstairs and spent a lot of time around my mother and her friends.

My mother and I were very close. We spent a lot of time together. We talked a lot.

We lived in a middle-class brick house in a middle-class suburban neighborhood of Reading, Pennsylvania. We were Catholic. We were hard-line Catholics, too. We'd go to church every Sunday, have our prayers before dinner, and say our rosaries during Lent. I went to a Catholic grade school and then on to Central Catholic High School (in the Luden's Mansion, as in Luden's Cough Drops). I was even an altar boy in my early teens.

My dad made about $40,000 a year, which was good money back then. We didn't drive around in a Mercedes or fly to Europe, but we were comfortable and we never had financial problems.

My dad started out with a luncheonette, and then sold that and started buying up insurance agencies and real estate companies. That's what he did for the rest of his life.

Dad was the opposite of my mother. He was half German, half Polish. His father was a strict man who felt that children were better seen and not heard. Like his father before him, my dad was strict with me. Once I turned thirteen, that ceased to work.

My father owned his own business, and he was

home for dinner every single work day at 6:00 p.m. I've wondered since how anyone with his own business can do that. You'd think that some days it would be impossible – that things would come up. But my father made it work. His life was structured so that he'd leave work at 5:00 p.m., go to the store to get anything my mom would need, and be home by 6:00 p.m. when we'd eat dinner. Every single day from Monday through Friday!

It was at dinner that everything happened and everything was said. It seemed we'd never talk to my dad unless we did it at the dinner table. He was almost like the Godfather. He got home just in time for dinner. We'd talk during dinner. Then after dinner he'd sit down with his newspaper and after that he'd go to bed. Except on the nights Mom had parties, that was it. His life was his work.

I vowed I would never be like that.

A Round Peg in a Square-Holed Society

For dinner, everyone sat down at the table in the same chairs at 6:00 p.m. every night. It never varied. Once in awhile I would come in early and sit down in someone else's chair just to drive them crazy. They'd come in, sit down, and realize something was wrong. Out of place. Then it would hit them that I was in somebody else's chair, and they'd tell me to get back where I belonged. It was as if I had disrupted the order of the universe.

The trouble with telling me to get back where I belonged was that I didn't really know where I belonged. Even back then it was becoming more and more obvious to me that I *didn't* fit in my family. I was too active, too energetic, too willing to step over the boundaries of the accepted standards and norms that had been set up.

It wasn't that I was doing anything bad. Just different. I just didn't fit – except with my mother, perhaps. She generally ended up defending me and pacifying my dad for me.

I wasn't trying to be a rebel. I wasn't trying to be *anything* except who I was. And who I was was different than who they were.

The chairs, for instance ... I thought it was the most ridiculous thing in the world to have to sit in the same chair at dinner every night. But it was a big thing to my family. I mean, what difference did it make where we sat? I guess they wanted that standard, that rigid structure. It was a form of comfort and complacency. It was like they wanted everything to be the same and never vary, so they wouldn't have to think about it.

My father was like that perhaps more than anyone else in the family. It was like he was saying, "This is what I do. This is where I work. This is where I live. I leave work at 5:00 p.m. every night. We eat dinner at 6:00 p.m. every night." And so on.

When I was young, my parents used to take me to doctors to try to get them to give me medication for being hyperactive. But the doctors would say, "You've just got a kid with a tremendous amount of energy. Leave him alone." Fortunately, the doctors wouldn't give them the medication, or I'd have been like Jack Nicholsen at the end of *One Flew Over the Cuckoo's Nest* – walking around like a zombie.

I didn't find any early allies in my siblings, either. I had two older sisters and one younger brother. My sisters were three and four years older than me, and my brother was three years younger. I think being close to two older sisters and a Sicilian mother helped shape my personality. I didn't have an older brother figure that I wanted to be like. I didn't have to be rough and tough. I had to be more in tune with how people *felt*. A lot of my sensitivity springs from that, I think. But it also pulled me even further away from the norm.

I had problems growing up with my oldest sister that widened the gap between me and the rest of the family. JoAnn was the most loved and revered child of the family. She was the first, and she was a girl and she could do no wrong. If she ever did anything wrong, Dad would say "She's got a lot of stress and pressure because she's the oldest."

One night at dinner my dad said something to her and she got mad. Really mad. First, she took God's name in vain – we were never, ever allowed to even use "bad" words, much less take the Lord's name in vain. Then she took her plate of spaghetti and threw it in Dad's face!

Guess what he did? Absolutely nothing! He didn't even get up. He just took his napkin, wiped off his face, got her some more spaghetti, and went on eating like nothing had happened. I was dumbfounded. I sat there thinking, "Am I watching a movie? Is this real? Is it really happening? Am I crazy?"

You can imagine the bewildered look on my face. I put my arms up and I said, "What is happening in this family?" And they looked at me like "What do you mean?" And I said, "Am I the only one that saw this? Didn't anyone see what just happened here?" Of course, my other sister and my brother didn't say a word. Neither did my mother. But my father just sat there and gave me a look that said, "What are you talking about?" And he never, ever mentioned a word about that incident. To this day, I still can't believe it! And of course, no one else seems to remember it!

Like I said, my sister JoAnn was the favorite. She could do things or say things to my father that he didn't like, and all she'd have to do is give him a hug and say, "You're the greatest!" and he'd be ready to buy her the world. If you have an idol, and that idol does something wrong, you don't see it as something wrong. That's the way my father was with my oldest sister. She could do something wrong and if you asked him if he saw it as being something wrong, he'd say, "Oh, that didn't really happen."

I remember we'd sometimes sit around and watch TV. I used to stretch out on the floor. When JoAnn had to get up for something, she'd walk across the room, and instead of just stepping over me, she'd drag her back foot and kick me. She knew that I'd say something and make a scene, and then she'd say to my mother, "I don't know why he's doing that." She just did it to irritate me and to push herself further up the ladder. I have to laugh when I think about it now, because she's really a wonderful person and we get along very well now. In fact, whenever we go to Reading, Pennsylvania, my wife, Kelly, and I stay with her and her husband, John, and their children, Alex, Ryan, and Ashley. Ashley is a doll, and the boys are great. I love staying there.

But growing up, we couldn't have been more different. You see, JoAnn was a politician – something that I never was. At least 99.5 percent of the time she'd play the game. She conformed. She always said the right thing. She always acted the right way. And she got away with everything.

I was the exact opposite. My father used to play a

tape called *The Attitude Tape* at the dining room table to try to get me to improve my attitude. I'll never forget it. Of course, he thought my attitude was bad. But all I was doing was saying what I thought, while JoAnn was saying what he wanted to hear. All I had to do is say what I thought, and if it was contrary to what they thought, I was the bad guy.

Even in school I was not your run-of-the-mill conformist. I always had a girlfriend going through school, so I never really "hung out" with the guys. Sure, I was in all the sports growing up – football, basketball, baseball, wrestling, and all that – but I wasn't into getting together with the guys all the time. I never really had a peer group at school because I always did what I wanted to do and went my own way. Still, I could be "popular" without having to go do the things that the other guys were doing.

My peer group was really my mother's friends. Those were the people I really liked being around. To sit around and talk with kids my own age at school was boring in comparison.

Because I didn't feel the need to conform to a peer group of my age bracket, I avoided a lot of the pressures and problems most kids go through. I never drank or smoked. I didn't need to swear. I didn't need to dress a certain way. I mean, I was an altar boy who was also a "jock." That wasn't the thing to do!

But then, doing "the thing to do," was never my way.

Energy and Entrepreneurship

It was 3:15 a.m. and my coat didn't keep out the brutal early morning cold. The truck that dropped off my newspapers every day was a few minutes late and I was indignant. It was inconceivable to my 12-year-old mind that anyone could be late for something this important. After all, this paper route was my key to unlimited wealth and prosperity. Now that I was 12 and qualified to have my very own route, I knew I could get everything I wanted in life.

I was an entrepreneur at an early age. I sold seeds – flower and vegetable seeds – door-to-door when I was eight. They used to advertise in the magazines that you could sell the seeds and make your dime profit and build up points to redeem for toys. I remember I got a bicycle.

I also started delivering newspapers at the age of eight. Since I couldn't have my own route until I was 12, I worked with my next-door neighbor. He lived directly across the street from me. I'd get him up at 5:00 a.m. in the morning to go deliver newspapers. Here I was, eight years old, and I was getting up every morning before this 12-year-old and dragging him out of bed so we could go out and make money.

When I turned 12, I got my own route, which was

the greatest present I could ever imagine. I was as thrilled as a kid could be. I saw that route as being the ticket to all the good things in life. I was so excited that I would get up at 3:30 a.m. every morning and be there waiting when the delivery truck dropped off the newspapers.

I'd deliver all the papers, then go home and go back to bed. When I'd get back up to go to school, it was like I never even did my paper route.

Collecting subscription money was a big part of a paper boy's job back then. Now they just send out bills and you pay them by mail. But back then we had to go to each door and collect the money in person and punch a little card showing that they had paid.

Anyway, the guy whose paper route I took over was sort of a long-haired hippie type. I was surprised he even had a route. He hardly ever went out collecting – just for a couple of hours each month after school when it was convenient for him.

When I got his paper route, I collected $500 in back payments *my first week*. I saw this as an incredible opportunity. But in order to make it happen, I had to go out collecting not only during the day, but on weekends and even at night to catch the business people who were never home during the day.

I loved that paper route. And I discovered a secret while I was doing it that has helped me ever since. I realized, as Brian Tracy says, that "if you can turn your work into a game, you can spend the rest of your life playing."

Getting up at 3:30 every morning to deliver papers

wasn't a hardship for me. In fact, it didn't even feel like a job because I turned it into a game. The game was throwing newspapers, and the goal was to make each paper I threw land precisely on the door mat.

I got so good at it that about 95 percent of the newspapers that I threw landed directly on the mats. That didn't happen right away, of course. It's just like a pitcher on a baseball team. If you throw thousands of balls, you're eventually going to be able to throw a lot of strikes. So that's what I'd do with my paper route. It became a game, a goal, a challenge for me each day, and I looked forward to it in the same way a good dart player looks forward to a dart game.

I played that game for the next five or six years, and only gave it up when I hit the maximum age that they let kids deliver papers.

It's possible to turn just about any type of work into play. I remember fixing up a house in New York. It had a driveway that needed to be dug up. Now, that's about as tough a job as there is. So I got a pickup truck, dug up the whole driveway with a pick and a shovel, and hauled it away. But I made it fun. I said, "Shoot, this is like lifting weights all day long. It's a great workout!"

Gardening was another entrepreneurial venture of my youth. I used to weed gardens and cut grass. There was a retired attorney who lived around the block from me who hired me to take care of his yard. His name was Mr. William George. He took a liking to me, and I liked him and looked up to him. In fact, he was probably my first mentor. He'd spend time talking to me about business and other things of life. I'd look forward to coming home from school so that I could go work at his house.

One day he said, "John, you're a good worker. I'll tell you what I'd like to do. You tell me what you want, and I'll get it for you."

I said, "What do you mean?"

He said, "Well, if you want a bike, or a stereo, or whatever – you tell me what you want. I'll buy it for you and you can work it off."

I thought about it and came back to him the next day and said I wanted a punching bag. So he bought me a $75 punching bag and I worked it off.

I used to shovel snow, too, starting from the time I was in grade school. I did it all the way through high school. I'd go out when snow storms would close the schools and make between $200 and $250 a day! The minute I'd found out that the school was closed, I'd grab my shovel and start knocking on doors. I knew that every half hour someone would say yes, and I'd make anywhere from $10 to $20. I'd do their walks and their driveways, and I'd do it all day long – ten hours a day.

The problem I had was that I couldn't get anyone else to do it with me. I loved to work, but enjoyed it so much more if I had a friend to do it with. My brother would help me for a few hours, then he'd go home because he was tired. Everyone saw the day as an opportunity to sleep in or go sledding. But I saw it as an opportunity to get ahead – not to sit around and relax and be lazy, but as a money-making opportunity.

It wasn't easy, of course. And sometimes it wasn't

pleasant. Some people would say no and some people would slam the door. But I never got upset because I knew that in 30 minutes someone was going to say yes and I was going to have another $10 bill or $20 bill in my pocket. That kept me going.

This venture, along with the experience of selling seeds, helped me to forever overcome the fear of rejection, and to believe in myself. I think everyone should have the education and experience that comes with door-to-door sales.

I'll admit it – I loved making money even back then. I mean, $200 is a fortune when you're a 14-year-old kid! I bought a stereo, a bike, models ... money went a long way in those days, which was good, because after I'd build an expensive model, my brother and I, for fun, would light it on fire or smash it against a wall. And when we'd get mad at each other, we'd run around smashing each other's models wherever we could find them. So my expenses were high.

I also painted houses. I did this all through high school. I'd go door-to-door up and down my street. I lived on a four-lane avenue with a grass strip down the middle. It was a busy road, and a long one. I would knock on doors to find houses to paint. I ended up doing five or six houses on the same street, and got about $500 a house. In the early to mid '70s, that was a fortune for a high school kid.

I've never grown out of my love for being a door-to-door entrepreneur.

Later in my life, I went door-to-door with a garage sale. This was after I got married, when I was about 21 or 22. It was just like a regular garage sale that you'd have in your driveway, but I went door-to-door. I pushed a lawn mower in front of me and carried a big basket. I'd knock on doors and say, "I'm having a garage sale, but instead of having you come to me, I'm coming to you. Would you like anything here?"

I ended up selling everything I wanted to sell – even the lawn mower. I remember the guy I sold it to. I knocked on his door, asked if he was interested, and he gave me ten $20 bills for it, which was exactly what I was asking.

People ask me why I'm so fond of going door-to-door. The fact is, it doesn't bother me, and there are a lot better odds going door-to-door than using other marketing methods.

On some of the television and radio talk shows I was on, they asked me what motivated me at such an early age to make money and do things that other people didn't normally do. I've really had to think about that, and the only answer that I can come up with is that kids usually either become what they are around growing up, or they become *the opposite*.

My family was a regular, normal, middle-income family. They didn't really stand out. They didn't buck the system. They conformed. It's not that there's anything wrong with that, but *I* didn't want it. I wanted more out of life. And I found that by doing things that my friends and my brother didn't want to do – like getting out on a snowy day and knocking on doors – I could get way ahead of the game.

And getting ahead of the game has always been a

thrilling experience for me.

The Sins of the Fathers

Sitting there at the dinner table – a kid filled with adolescent traumas and problems and dreams – I realized how very much I needed my father to talk to me, to listen to me, one-on-one. But as I watched him there at the head of the table, isolated by the cloud of rigid authority that seemed to always surround him, I knew that would never happen, and I felt a hole burn through my insides that I would spend the rest of my life trying to fill.

The older I get, the more I realize how deeply a child's relationship with his parents affects him throughout his life.

I know this from painful personal experience. My relationship with my dad was not horrible. But it was not the best, either. Outwardly, we probably appeared to have quite a normal father-son relationship.

We had gotten along well when I was younger. He'd take me hunting and we'd do that sort of dad-and-son thing. But once I turned into a teenager and had a girlfriend and my own opinions, that's when the tides turned.

One experience – one I can't forget – helps illustrate what I'm saying. My father was not a talker. You couldn't talk to him about anything that had anything to do with your reality. His life was his work. This was tough because I really needed and wanted a father I could talk to, someone who really cared about me, and showed it the way I wanted to see it. I never felt like I got that.

He was a great man, but he wasn't what I wanted. Of course, I wasn't what he wanted, either. And we both let each other know.

Anyway, I remember coming home after my first semester of college. Dad was sitting on the front porch reading his newspaper. I sat down next to him and started talking about what was going on at school. I was really trying to open up to him. Suddenly, without saying a word, he just stood up and walked into the house.

I couldn't believe it! Here I was trying to talk to him – which I'd always had a tough time doing – and treating him like he was the father I wanted him to be, and he just got up and walked away. Never said a word! I sat there on the porch and cried.

It wasn't until later in life that I began to understand why my father was like he was. I found out from my mother that Dad's father never talked to him. He was a hard, stern German. He had strict rules, made his children do things, and never allowed them to disagree. Ever. Growing up, Dad was never even allowed to make it known that he thought differently about something. So naturally, that's what Dad wanted from me. And that was our problem.

Of course, I didn't know any of this until the damage had been done. And frankly, I'm not sure that knowing it at the time would have made things any better.

Here's another illustration of how Dad's strong, silent father image impacted our relationship: Back in high school, when I was about 15, I would hitchhike to my girlfriend's house. She lived about three miles away, and we used to both start walking toward each other's house at the same time, so that we'd meet halfway. But when I could, I liked to hitchhike and get dropped off behind her, then surprise her by running up to her from the opposite direction.

One Saturday afternoon, a state cop (who must have had a real bad day) pulled up alongside me on the road. Here I was, a clean-cut suburban high school kid hitchhiking two miles to my girlfriend's house. For some reason (all the kids hitchhiked around there), he said he wanted me to go with him.

Being the cocky high school wrestler that I was, I said, "No! What do you want me to get in the car for?" The cop said, "Just get in the car." I said no again. So he pulled his car up and cut me off, like one of those movies where they pull in front of a car to stop it. But I was walking!

He jumped out of his car – state cops have to be at least six feet tall, and this guy looked bigger than that – and grabbed me by the arm. I swatted his arm off. Then he went for his handcuffs, and I swatted those away. It was like he was crazy. I yelled, "What are you doing?" He grabbed me again. I must have had an incredible surge of adrenalin, because I picked him up and threw him onto the stairs that went up to a house. (I know this happened because the next day someone I knew told me he had driven by and seen it all.)

The cop lay there on the stairs for a few seconds. We were both stunned. I could see that his arm was a little bloody. Then he got up and put his hand on his gun. That's when I ran. I remember running in a zigzag pattern so if he tried to shoot me he'd miss. I had no idea what this crazy guy was going to do!

You've got to picture this. Here I am, a 15-year-old kid, scared out of my mind, running back to the refuge of my home and family. I ran into the house. My heart was pounding like crazy. I was breathing and talking real fast. I told my dad what happened. The cop pulled up.

Now, what do you think my dad said to the cop? He looked at me, then looked back at the cop and said coldly, "Take him away. He deserves it."

I just about had a nervous breakdown. I remember falling to the ground and crying my eyes out for what seemed to me to be a good 15 minutes.

And that's when things changed for me. I said to myself, "I'm not going to let this happen. I'm *not* going to let this happen! This is what *he* wants. He wants to have control over me."

I stood up and went down to the sheriff's office with the cop. Fortunately, the state cop's superior officer was there. He looked at me, looked at the cop, I told him what had happened, and he reprimanded the cop. I've always been treated fairly by the legal system, and this was the beginning. Anytime I've had trouble, all I had to do was tell the truth, and everything worked out.

This traumatic experience made me realize that I was on my own, that I had only myself to rely on. I mean, who else is there if you don't have your parents? That's when I knew that I had to be completely independent.

Another time while I was in college, I came home for a visit. I was 17 years old. Up until that point in my life, I accepted what my parents would say. Sure, I'd tell them exactly what I thought about things, but I'd basically do what they told me to do. If they made me stay home or something like that, I'd say something about it, but I'd do what I was told.

During that visit, Dad got on me as if I were a kid again. It was more than I could take, and I lost my temper. We were in the basement, sitting on the couch. I stood up. "Dad," I said, "don't stand up." Because I knew if he stood up we'd have a problem. He started to get up.

I put my hand on his chest and gently eased him back down onto the couch. Again I said, "Dad, *don't get up.*" Fortunately, he didn't, and it ended there. That was the closest we ever came to a fist fight.

I was so upset, though, that I stormed upstairs to go to my girlfriend's house. Just as I got to the top of the steps, my sister JoAnn, who I guess had heard the confrontation and wanted to chalk up some "Brownie points," literally jumped at me like a crazed cat. When I put out my hands to protect myself and push her back, she fell back against the refrigerator, crumpled onto the floor, and pretended that she was knocked out, which of course gave her some real serious points with our parents.

All I could think of was to get out of that house, which I did. I didn't even stop to put my shoes on. I remember I had to go down to a neighbor's house and borrow a pair so I could get to my girlfriend's place.

I don't want to give the impression that our home life was always like this. This incident was the worst blow-up I ever had at home. Usually, things were placid and controlled. But the experience sheds some light on some of the dynamics underlying our relationships.

I am only now beginning to realize how deeply my relationship with my father – or lack of it – has impacted me, and shaped my personality.

For example, I have always found it difficult to deal with authority figures, such as the police. I've already mentioned the hitchhiking incident. But there were two other incidences. One happened early in my married life. My wife and I and the two kids we had at the time were out doing some errands one day. I dropped them off at a corner grocery store to do some shopping, and I went on down the block to get gas. I pumped $10 worth into my car, went to pay, and the guy told me I owed $20.

What happened was that the particular pump I was using was the only pump at that station that hadn't been switched over to the new three-digit displays for the higher gas prices. On the pump I was using, you were supposed to double the price on the display. But they'd taken down the sign and I didn't know that.

The problem was that I only had $10 with me. I said, "Look, I'm going home to get the $10, because I don't have it here with me." The attendant looked at my expensive car and I suppose he thought that anyone driving a car like that *must* have lots of money in his pocket. So he didn't want me to leave until I coughed up the extra $10.

The whole situation was ridiculous. We got into a verbal confrontation, and finally I just took off, picked up my wife and kids, and headed home to get the money.

Before I got home, the cops pulled me over. The guy at the gas station had actually called the police! The officer told me I had to go with him. He was a young guy with a real "gung ho" attitude. I felt like smacking him because at that time in my life, I had that kind of attitude, too. (Isn't it funny how you pick up on things in other people that you have in yourself?)

Anyway, he told me to get in his car, and I said, "Hey, you're never going to be able to get me to go in that car, so don't even try." Well, he called some back-up units and they ended up taking me away. Fortunately, my uncle, who was Italian, knew some people and got me out of it. Nothing ever came of it.

The other run-in with the police happened when I was living in a town house in New York. The Moonies, which were big back then, came into our town house complex selling butterflies at ten o'clock *at night*. There was a "No Soliciting!" sign, but they didn't pay any attention to it. So I called the cops. They came over, got the Moonies out, and told me to call them if they ever came again.

They came again with their butterflies. This time, I kept the Moonie in my house, saying, "I'm calling the cops on you. You don't have your license, and you're going to wait here until they come to take you away." Moonies are really laid back, so this guy just stood there and waited.

I called the cops and a few minutes later an officer walked right into my house – didn't even knock – and said, "You call the police?"

This guy must have been six feet tall and 300 pounds! He looked like a big, overblown member of a motorcycle gang that had somehow been squeezed into a cop's uniform.

He walked in, ignoring me altogether, sat down and started looking at the butterflies, and said, "Oh, wow! These butterflies are really nice. I'm really glad you called me, sir! Thanks for making me come all the way up here just for this. I never would have been able to experience these butterflies if it wasn't for you!" He was as arrogant as they get.

I said, "*What* are you doing?"

And he said, "I'm looking at the butterflies. Do you have a problem with that?"

I didn't say anything else. I just stood there and watched him in amazement.

A few minutes later the back-up cop knocked on the door and came in very politely. He was a younger, inexperienced guy. He asked me what was going on. I said, "You know, I'd like to know that, too. I think your partner is drunk. I'd like you to give him a sobriety test."

When I said that, the big cop stood up, walked over to me like he was going to twist my head off, and said, "You got a problem with me?"

So, of course, I said, "Yeah, as a matter of fact, I *do* have a problem with you. I don't like the way you're handling this."

So he said, "Are you telling me you don't like the way I'm handling this *investigation*?"

"Right."

"Well, then why don't you step outside and file a complaint?"

So I followed him out. He was standing at the bottom of the two steps in front of my place, and I was standing at the top. Suddenly, he grabbed me to throw me down on the ground. I was completely surprised, but I had learned how to keep my balance in wrestling, so when he tried to throw me down, I grabbed the shoulders of his leather jacket, picked my legs up, and it was like we were doing a dance.

He yelled to his partner, "Resisting arrest!" and they cuffed me and took me away!

When I got to the station, they basically just let me go. I was furious, but I couldn't mess around with it, because I had my insurance license at the time and if I had any kind of a record, I'd lose it. But just a couple of months later, I found out that the same cop had roughed up somebody, and the person he roughed up won $35,000 in a lawsuit against the city.

I'm not a law-breaker. And I'm certainly not a criminal. That's why I have trouble making sense of the unpleasant situations I've had with the police and certain other authority figures. I have a feeling that a good psychoanalyst would trace it all back to my relationship with my father. Unfortunately, it was a relationship that I'll never be able to completely heal.

As I said before, my dad's life was his work, and he did well in providing financially for our family. Eventually, he merged insurance businesses with a father and son team. They each had bought about six or seven insurance agencies. They merged and did business together for six or seven years.

After that amount of time, my dad was very content with the business as it was. He was happy. He didn't want to take any risks and didn't want to expand. But my dad's younger partner – the son – wanted to expand. He was younger and more aggressive. He wanted more money. He wanted more out of the business. So one day he told my father that he wasn't going to give him a paycheck anymore.

That hit my dad hard. In fact, it killed him – literally. You see, his whole life was built around his work. Most of his good friends were his clients. When he was forced out of his business, his whole physical system shut down, he got cancer, and in six months, at the age of 58, he was dead.

Before Dad realized he was ill, I called him to ask if he wanted to spend a weekend with me at Pine Hill or Pine Crest, or somewhere on the East Coast where the golfing was incredible. Knowing Dad, I figured there was no way he would say yes, even though I was paying for everything and he had wanted to do this for years.

To my astonishment, and my family's, Dad said yes without hesitation. We started making plans. Just a few weeks before our golf trip, he found out he had cancer and couldn't go. But he had said yes. He had actually wanted to go with me. That was the beginning of a brief period of time during which he was the father I had always wanted him to be.

As Dad got progressively worse, my brother and sisters wanted to pretend he would get better. Denial is an interesting thing. When I went to see him for a brief visit a few month's before his death, I couldn't believe anyone thought he would ever get up again.

It was then that I knew it was time to set his business, will, and so forth in order. But I couldn't get my family to help do it, because that would force them to face the reality of his situation. After numerous struggles over the telephone, I finally decided to go spend some time with Dad and help the family deal with this.

It worked But it also turned out to be the best thing I could have done for myself, because Dad and I got so close during that time. He couldn't get out of bed alone, so I helped him. It was like we had reversed roles. I was there for him to the end. We held each other and talked like we'd never done before. Something inside me told me to stay at home with him a little longer than I had planned. The reason was that he would pass away in just a few more days.

I remember one day Dad asked me what he should do. I asked him what he meant by that. He said, "About hanging on." He couldn't eat or drink anymore. He was incapable of going to the bathroom. He had dropped from 200 to 85 pounds in six months. I said, "Dad, Mom is okay. Your mother is okay. We're all okay. It's time to stop worrying about everyone else and think of yourself. You can let go now. Everything will be okay."

You see, he had been trying so hard to believe what they were telling him about his condition, yet he knew it was over for him. He was in horrible pain, yet he was still struggling to hang on.

I remember crying that night because now, at the end of his life, he had become the father I had always wanted him to be, and it seemed I had become the son he had always wanted.

One day later, Dad died in peace. We were all there holding his hands when he took his last breath – Mom, his mother, my brother and sisters, me, our spouses. I felt his spirit leave his body. It was a moment unlike any I will probably ever experience again in my life – a moment of intense joy and spirituality. I thank God for the opportunity I had to be with him then.

If only we could have started that kind of relationship earlier! But I know we'll continue where we left in the next life.

All or Nothing

When I'd wrestle my matches and pin somebody, they'd take pictures afterward. If you were to see those pictures, you'd think I was the one that lost. They always had to help me off the mat. I put every ounce of energy into each match. I had nothing on my mind except pinning my opponent. And when it was over, I had nothing left to give.

I've taken an "all or nothing" approach to life as long as I can remember. It's just the way I am. If I do something, I do it all the way, with all my energy. If I like people, I like them completely, without reservation. If I think something or feel something, I don't try to hide it.

This hasn't always made my life easy. But then, I haven't had much choice in the matter. I was made a certain way, and to try to stifle who I am would not only be a betrayal of myself, but would likely be impossible.

Besides, my all-or-nothing way of living has yielded some excellent results, even though it's often a tough road to follow. My wrestling career is a good example.

When I wrestled in high school, I broke every record there was to break. As a kid, I was strong and fairly big. I had a 42-inch chest when I was in ninth grade. (Now I'm just under six feet tall and I have a 50-inch chest.) One of the reasons I was strong as a kid was that I worked. When you're shoveling snow, cutting lawns, and carrying 40-foot ladders around to paint houses, you can't help but get strong.

I pinned every opponent I wrestled my senior year, except one. And the reason I didn't pin him was because I had a 104-degree temperature the day we wrestled. I'll never forget that match. I had him on his back three times, but I was too weak and sick to hold him tight enough to get the pin. Still, I beat him 15 to 3.

I was successful in wrestling because I gave it everything I had, and then some. I was in the 185-pound wrestling class. There was a guy named Phil in the 167-pound class. He and I would always wrestle together in practices. One day someone visited one of our workouts from another school. He came up to us afterwards and said, "You guys wrestle like it's the national championships!"

I thought about that. It was true. We put everything we had into it. We didn't know the names of the moves. We weren't incredibly talented on a technical level. But we put our hearts into it. When we got done wrestling, I'd go home, eat dinner, and go to bed. I was literally exhausted.

I was supposed to get the Athlete of the Year Award at the last assembly of school. The entire school was in the assembly hall, and I was getting all kinds of trophies for the most pins and other records I'd broken in wrestling. But when it came time to award me the Athlete of the Year Award, nothing happened. It was like they had completely forgotten about it.

Naturally, I was disappointed. After the assembly when I walked outside to go home, the school's athletic director, Mr. Jones, walked up to me and casually handed me the Athlete of the Year Award trophy. "Oh, by the way John," he said, "you won this."

Later, I found out what had happened. Mr. Jones had a brother that was in my class. When I first got to high school in ninth grade, I wanted to play basketball. The basketball coach at that time was Mr. Jones. His brother went out for the team, too, and he started him instead of me. I knew I was better than his brother. I loved basketball, but I couldn't do anything about it. So I quit the team and went into wrestling.

When it was time to select the recipient of the Athlete of the Year Award, Jones came back to haunt me. He tried to lobby the other coaches to vote for his brother instead of me. Although his brother was a nice kid, he just wasn't that talented of an athlete, and the other coaches wouldn't go along with him and selected me. But since his brother hadn't won, Jones wouldn't give me the trophy during the assembly.

I was mad, but I got over it in a few hours. I just thought, "Hey, that guy's got to live with himself for the rest of his life. I'm lucky – I don't have to deal with him anymore."

Being completely up-front and outspoken is another facet of my all-or-nothing personality that has made life difficult at times. (Don't get me wrong – I don't regret the way I am. I'd much rather be totally up-front and outspoken than be the kind of "politician" that says whatever the crowd wants to hear.)

But I *did* pay a stiff price occasionally for refusing to say what others wanted to hear. Baseball was one "payment" I made.

I loved baseball in grade school. And I loved my coach, Charlie K. He was fabulous. He had been a pitcher for the Cleveland Indians. When he met his wife, he was driving a pink convertible Corvette with polka dots. I love people who aren't afraid to be different, who don't feel like they have to conform.

I was a good pitcher and I had over a 400 batting average. Then I went into ninth grade and went out for baseball. The coach cut me from the lineup. At first I couldn't believe it. Then I figured it out. He didn't like me, and I didn't like him. He was a jerk – the kind of guy you had to totally kiss up to and say, "Oh, almighty Coach," if you wanted to play. And I refused to do that. So I quit and didn't play baseball all during high school. That's another reason why I ended up wrestling.

In college I had a finance class. In one of the first classes, the teacher asked for any comments. I raised my hand and stood up. "Professor," I said, "you told us one of your goals is to teach us how to make millions of dollars. How can you ride a bicycle to school and dress like that if you know how to make money?" I realize now that that wasn't the nicest thing to say, and I hadn't said it to put him down. It's just that I really wanted an answer, because I didn't feel like it was worth listening to someone who hadn't done what he was trying to teach others how to do. I got kicked out of that class.

All through school, I just couldn't be a politician. I

had to say what I thought. When I liked people, they knew it. I'd wash their car for them. I'd do anything for them. It was that way with my wrestling coach, who gave me all the support and incentive I needed. We had a great relationship. I liked him and he liked me and I broke records for him.

But when I didn't like someone, they knew that, too. I wouldn't give them the time of day. Consequently, throughout most of my school career I'd get A's and B's if I liked the teacher, and C's and D's if I didn't. And I'd often get D's and F's in self-control. I would say what I thought, and my teachers considered it a lack of self-control. But I thought it was *total control.*

I became a fighter about the time I was feeling the most rejected by my father. And, true to form, when I fought, I'd let it all out.

I think I got the idea that fighting was okay back in the second grade. There was a kid who sat behind me who would write on my shirt with a pen. It really upset me. I remember crying on my way home, knowing my parents would get mad because I was always putting holes in my clothes and tearing them anyway.

So one night at dinner, when I told them about this, my dad said, "Look, if that guy writes on your shirt again tomorrow, this is what I want you to say to him: 'My father told me that I'm supposed to punch you in the nose if you write on my shirt again.' Use those exact words."

That's exactly what I did. The next day I went to school, sat down in my home room class, and he started writing on my shirt again.

I turned around. I was terrified. My heart was pounding. I said, "My dad told me that I'm supposed to punch you in the nose if you write on my shirt again."

The kid thought I was joking and started writing on my shirt. I stood up in the middle of class, turned around, and punched him in the nose. I'll never forget how his white shirt – it was a Catholic school and we all had to wear white shirts – got completely covered with blood.

The teacher grabbed me and took me down to the principal's office. I was crying. I told them that he'd been writing on my shirt, and that my dad told me to punch him in the nose if he did it again, and that I had to do what my dad told me to do. They said, "Okay." I didn't get in trouble. And I didn't hear another word about it.

When I was in ninth and tenth grades, fighting became a way of life for me. I must have a hundred scars on my hands from those days. That was when I used to tell people that I hated my dad because he wanted me to be a certain way, and I didn't want to be that way.

It was obvious that Dad was disenchanted with me. I took all the hurt, frustration, and anger that this triggered in me out on bullies. I was almost like a vigilante from the Old West. If I felt like someone needed a lesson, I would give it to him. For instance, there was a guy that came to our school from a public school. He was a proverbial bully type – like the guy that comes into a small town from the big city and walks around with big boots and a leather jacket and creates trouble. In short, a real creep.

So I challenged him to a fight. I walked up to him one day and said, "Look, I don't like you. I want to fight you." We scheduled it for the next day down at the city park. I brought a change of clothes that day and changed in the locker room after school. By the time I got down to the park, there were at least 200 people waiting to see the fight. I won.

But then, I always won. In all my fights, not only did I never lose, I never even got hit! Looking back, I realize now that it would have been good for me to have taken a good punch on the nose or gotten hurt just once.

But I was very aggressive and cocky, and I didn't get punched, so I kept fighting. Consequently, I almost got kicked out of school, and I was on the skids academically.

Then something happened that changed everything. One day during the summer after tenth grade, I was playing basketball with a good friend of mine, Chuck. He really took a risk. He said, "John, do you think people like you fighting?"

I asked him what he meant. After all, I only beat up bullies that deserved it (or that *I* thought deserved it), I pointed out.

He said, "But *you're* deciding who's good and who's bad."

I actually had never thought about that! It hit me like the punch to the nose I'd never taken. Everyone wants people to like them, and I was no exception. I always thought the other kids liked what I was doing, but what I didn't realize was that I was pushing people away from me because they were afraid.

From that day on I never got in another fight (and to this day never have and never will). Everything went better. I went from a C+ average in ninth and tenth grades to straight A's in the eleventh and twelfth grades. I was on the honor roll. The teachers loved me. I got along great with the other students. My whole life changed when Chuck told me what I needed to hear. I'll always be grateful to him for taking the risk – for being honest and outspoken, and not being a politician. To this day, whenever I go back to my hometown, I look him up and we have lunch or dinner. He's a successful attorney now.

Even though I was on the honor roll during my last two years of high school, the faculty wouldn't graduate me on the honor roll because of my lack of performance during my ninth and tenth grade years – even though my overall average was high enough.

But there was another reason. Although most of my teachers loved me – at least during those last two years – there were a few who didn't because I had insulted them by telling them exactly what I thought. (They deserved to be insulted – or so I thought, at least.) Anyway, they never forgave me.

It's like politics. In politics, you never burn bridges. But of course I *always* burned bridges.

Looking for My Niche

*Early in my job I figured something out.
The other guys all knocked on 75 doors a day
and were making about $20,000 a year. It
stood to reason that if I knocked on 150 doors
a day, I could make $40,000 a year. So I did.
I was making $40,000 a year selling siding door-
to-door!*

After high school I went to college for a year at
Westchester State in Westchester, Pennsylvania – about
a 45-minute drive from Reading. I knew I was going to
work for my dad and eventually take over his part of the
business or work on my own. I'd always been an entrepreneur. I knew I could do my own thing. So I went to
college for a year (I lived in a dorm there in Westchester), paid my way, took a whole bunch of business
classes, and that was it.

I worked for my dad for about a year after that.
But it didn't work out. Again, I was a nonconformist. I
wanted to expand and make the business more than
what it was. Dad was comfortable with the business the
way it was, and wanted to maintain the status quo.
Before I had been on the payroll for a year, I quit.

It was during the time I worked for Dad in the
insurance business that I met Tracy. We got to know

each other at Aetna Insurance school in Hartford where she worked. I was taking an insurance class there. She was young, nice, and stood 5'-2". We were married in 1978. Nine months later, we had our first child. I was only 20 years old, but having children while I was still young was one of my goals in life.

After we were married, her father, Bob, made me an offer to come and work at his siding business in Rochester, New York. (Her mom had been married three times, so she didn't carry his name. Her dad had been married three times, too.)

"Why don't you come up here for a week," he said. I'll pay your way and you can take a look at what I do. If you like it, I'll give you a job."

Bob is a man who quit school in sixth grade. He's not just brilliant – he's a literal genius. He remembers everything he reads. He was absolutely the most intelligent man I had ever met in my life to that point.

So I went up there for a week. It was February, there was a foot of snow on the ground, it was 20 degrees below with the wind-chill factor, and one of his sales people and I were out there going door-to-door selling siding.

These salespeople of his were just regular, everyday "Joes." They weren't executives. They weren't rocket scientists. They were just regular guys. But they were making $20,000 a year, which was a decent living in '79. In comparison, my father was paying me $15,000 a year.

I saw the opportunity and went back to Pennsylvania to tell my dad I was quitting. He thought I was crazy to go to New York chasing a commission-only job with a wife and a baby. But it didn't take me long to prove that I wasn't at all crazy. In fact, I was doing so well that Bob started talking to me about the possibility of opening up an office in Connecticut. (By working twice as hard, I was making twice as much money: $40,000 a year.)

But by then something had happened that made me change my views about the siding business. My wife and I had joined a different church, and had become active members of a congregation. The things I learned in church about dealing completely honestly with people made me reevaluate selling siding for a living because of the sales gimmicks that are used in that industry. I wasn't comfortable pretending that we were having a sale on siding when in reality there was no actual sale. We just tried to get what we could get. Even before joining the church, that had rubbed my sense of honesty the wrong way.

So I quit and we moved back to Pennsylvania. I didn't realize it at the time because he didn't say a word about it, but when I left the siding business and left Rochester, it *really* hurt my father-in-law. That was something I would not have done, had I known.

You see, Bob was a very special person to me. We hit it off from the start. We lived with him the first two months after we first moved to Rochester, and he and I worked out together both mornings and nights. He had his own weights in the basement, but had never done anything with them. When I found out that he really wanted to get into shape, but just needed a little motivation, I started working out with him twice a day. We also ran together. He soon got into shape.

While we were working out and running together, I would ask Bob questions about business. I bent his ear like crazy. It was a great relationship. We liked each other immensely. We respected each other. And we were giving each other what the other person needed.

Bob didn't get along with his own son – a kid that didn't care much about business or working – and it was like he adopted me as his own son. Looking back, I suppose at the same time I adopted him as my own father. We both had needs in those directions that hadn't been filled. Anyway, he thought I was the greatest, and the feeling was mutual.

So when I quit his business and went back to Pennsylvania – although *I* never thought it was a big deal – Bob was personally hurt because *he wanted to give the business to me*. He wanted me to follow in his footsteps. And he never told me this! Instead, he just said, "Hey, you've got to do what you've got to do." But inside, it tore him up.

Tracy and I and our child spent the next six months in Pennsylvania, where I did a lot of thinking about what I wanted to do with my life. I worked for my wonderful Sicilian uncle, Iggy, doing demolition work during that time. Finally, we decided that since we knew a lot of people back in Rochester, we'd move back there and I'd go into insurance. Which is what we did.

I got a job selling life insurance with New York Life. That's where I met Paul.

Paul had every license and title you could get in the insurance business. He was a professional student, was always studying, and in fact, was working on his masters degree when I met him. Consequently, he knew the insurance business inside and out. His knowledge was phenomenal.

On the other hand, he was insecure, had low self-esteem, and stuttered badly.

Paul was the sales trainer at our insurance company, but nobody liked him because of his speech problem. I got to be friends with him. He liked me because I was a maverick, and was the total opposite of him. I liked him because he was nice, because he talked to me, and because he wasn't in competition with me.

I've had a problem with this competition thing all my life. For instance, friends will come over and we'll shoot a friendly game of pool, and they get all wrapped up in winning. I want to say, "Hey, let's just have fun," but they're always trying to win. More often than not, *I'm* the one who wins. Same with tennis. I'll play tennis with friends, and they get tied up about winning and start complaining about how they're playing. So I don't play half as well as I *can* play because the other guy is getting depressed, and it's not fun for me. If you have to contend with a poor competitor's attitude, it takes the fun right out of the game.

That's one of the reasons Paul and I got along so well – we were two totally different types of people, and we could be ourselves without competing with each other. Paul was completely happy with knowing what he knew, and with me being myself completely.

We worked together so well that we started working with business people, selling big life insurance policies. People liked Paul because he was knowledgeable, and of course I'd do the sales part of it. We did so well together that I became the top insurance salesperson in our office. There was a guy who had been there over 20 years, and I broke all his records because I was working with Paul.

If I could get Paul in front of someone, that person appreciated his knowledge, and appreciated the fact that he wasn't just trying to sell – he was trying to give him what he really needed. I would sell the appointment, and I would sell him. Then he would come in like a professor, talking technically, and the policies would sell themselves. We made the perfect team.

What I did with Paul is what I've done throughout my life. I'll find a genuine person who has a lot of talent or skills or knowledge and create a win-win situation where that person can do what he's best at, I can do what I'm best at, and those two things complement each other.

With Paul, for example, I knew and he knew that I could do certain things well, and that he had a tremendous amount of talent and knowledge that I didn't have. I respected that and wouldn't cross the boundaries. He always knew that he could give me an idea, suggestion, or constructive criticism and I would accept it.

Having found someone who believed in him, confided in him, trusted him, and appreciated his talents, Paul came alive and we did phenomenal things together. I wasn't doing it just for the money's sake. I was doing it because Paul was great, and I didn't have any trouble telling him that, or vice versa.

Success at an Early Age

It was completely silent on the set. In a few seconds, the television cameras would start rolling. It occurred to me at that moment how lucky I was. Yes, it was a thrill to be a guest on yet another talk show to talk about my life and how I had made it "big." But what was even more of a thrill was realizing that I had built an incredibly happy and rewarding life – not only in business, but more importantly, on a personal and family level.

While working with Paul, I discovered that there were a lot of business people out there with a lot of money. I also found out that a huge percentage of them had it invested in real estate.

I went back and talked to one of these people about real estate – a man I had gotten to know through making an insurance proposal. He told me that real estate investing was the greatest thing in the world, and that I should start studying it.

That's when I got the book, *How to Wake Up the Financial Genius Inside You.* That was the start. The beginning. From then on, I started going to seminars and reading everything I could get my hands on about real estate.

I was so excited that I went out and began looking at hundreds of potential investment houses. But I didn't buy any because my wife feared any kind of debt. You see, she didn't live with her father growing up. She lived with her mother. And her mother was not wealthy. So she was deeply afraid of any kind of investment that would put us in debt. She didn't even want us to buy our own house.

So I just kept studying and looking at possible investment properties, and waiting for something to happen that would let me get started.

My patience paid off in 1982. The "something" that gave me my opportunity was not what I would have expected. It was a "peeping Tom." A guy was running around the town house complex where we lived, looking in windows and basically terrorizing the three town houses adjoining ours, because there were girls living there. It got so bad that the guy actually broke into our next-door neighbors' town house. That's when Tracy said, "We're moving."

I said, "Fine, we're moving. But we're moving into a house, and I know the perfect one to buy."

It was a single-family home with just a little over 1500 square feet. It was listed for $29,000. I offered $20,000 and they countered with $25,000. I was shocked! Why would anyone drop their price so much so fast? We settled on $23,500, with the sellers paying the closing costs and points. The Realtor said I needed $1,200 to close. I said no problem, and bought the house on my credit card (one of the many techniques I had learned from my studies).

I told the Realtor I needed some money to fix the house up, and she said she'd "build it into the cost of the house." As we walked out of the closing, she handed me a check for $2,500.

We improved the home. It was absolute fun for me! I got a reputation in our neighborhood as "that crazy guy who stays up all night working on his house."

There was a two-car garage at the back of the lot that I wanted to take out and replace with a yard. I dug up the driveway with a pick and shovel, hauled it off, then put an ad in the paper to sell the two steel garage doors (in excellent condition) for $2. The catch was that to get the doors, the buyer would have to tear down the garage and haul it away. I quickly found two guys who wanted the wood to heat their house. And since they didn't have jobs, they had the time to take down the garage and sell the doors.

I did a lot of work on that house. A friend of mine, Rick, came over one day to help me. We really hit it off. He loved doing that kind of work, and I loved the way he did it. I told him I was going to buy and fix up other properties and he said he'd like to help. That was the beginning of a beautiful relationship. I eventually hired Rick full-time and he became one of my most valuable business assets.

By the time I was finished with our house, I had put about $3,500 into fixing it up. With the initial cost, and taking the money I got back at closing into account, I had approximately $25,000 into the home. Because of the work we had done, it appraised for $40,000. We refinanced it for 85 percent of its value and pulled out about $10,000!

That was the beginning of my real estate career. I continued buying, fixing, up, and either selling, refinancing, or renting properties. It was a literal gold mine! By working hard and being smart, I could "turn" properties and make big profits in a short period of time. One property comes to mind in which I netted a $60,000 profit in a two-month period of time.

My method for finding the right properties was quite simple, but time-consuming. I would take the Sunday newspaper's classified ads for real estate and read through every one of them. If one sounded interesting, I'd call and fill out a property analysis sheet that I had designed.

I'd spend Monday through Wednesday calling and following up on the classified ads that I didn't get in touch with Sunday. Then I'd switch into the viewing phase, driving by each property that fit my criteria. If I thought a house had potential, I'd set up an appointment to see the interior. This was often frustrating, because many owners didn't show up, or came late. If, after looking at the inside of a house, I still thought it had potential, then I'd negotiate with the owners.

To many people, this process might seem very tedious. I'll admit, it was. But it paid off.

There was another method I used quite often: I'd revert to my old tactics and go out knocking on doors in a neighborhood, asking "Have you ever thought of selling your property?"

In both these methods, I was applying the same principal to real estate that I had used when I shoveled snow. I knew that if I got out and kept knocking on doors, I'd get a "sell" on the average of every half hour. In real estate, I knew that if I'd get out and look at 100 houses, I'd find at least a few that would turn excellent profits and make all my work more than worthwhile.

It wasn't long before I decided to quit my insurance career and go into real estate investing full time. I hired Rick as my full-time foreman, and we were on our way.

My career moved along like a meteor at this point. I brought partners and investors into some projects. I did more and more deals. And I began to "grow" a staff and an office. (Our office, in fact, was a good real estate investment purchase in and of itself.) I had a knack for looking past a property's problems and defects, and being able to see what *could be*.

I learned something very interesting during this period of my life: nothing is ever perfect, and if you wait for perfection, you're going to spend the rest of your life waiting. A good friend of mine named Stan and I would analyze properties together. But that's all he ever did. He never bought a single piece of real estate because nothing was perfect enough for him.

It was like Zig Ziglar says, "Some people won't back out of their driveways to go on a trip until all the lights are green." Stan was like that when it came to real estate investing. He had what I call the "paralysis of analysis." It paralyzed him. It stopped him from ever taking a chance.

My company was called J. Ross Development. As the business grew, I hired more and more people to keep up with the work until I had quite a large staff, including my own full-time attorney and accountant, both with assistants. Hiring an attorney turned out to be a good investment. With the cost of each closing and all the other legal work that had to be done, I would have paid an attorney more each year on a fee basis.

A regrettable incident took place about this time. A young entrepreneur (a swindler, actually), Tom T., got arrested in Rochester for getting a lot of people to invest in a gallery in Rochester, then taking the money and going to Europe. When he returned, he was arrested and went to jail. The whole thing got a lot of coverage in the press.

What did this have to do with me? Absolutely nothing. But unfortunately, the crook was my same age, looked a bit like me, and like me, was a good salesman and aggressive. I had some partners at the time in a few properties that suddenly wanted out. They had no apparent reason. The only thing I could come up with was that the incident somehow shook them up. Maybe they associated me with the swindler simply because we outwardly looked and acted alike in some ways. The main difference, of course, was that I would never do anything malicious or dishonest like he had done.

Those particular partners did get out of the partnership, and in the end, it worked out better for me financially. But it hurt me that they didn't know me better or have more trust in me.

As my company grew, I found that the only thing that was holding me back was cash. With more cash we could grow faster than ever. Mark, my new attorney, lived across the street from a man who was the top manager for the biggest real estate broker and mortgage broker in the area: John T. I got Mark to introduce me, and a few days and dinners later, I was the proud holder of a $250,000 line of credit. It was set up so that I could walk into Mr. T.'s office, give his secretary the purchase offer for a house, tell her how much I needed for repairs and boom! – I had the check.

I became somewhat of a celebrity during my rise to riches. The press got wind of what I was doing and I soon became their "pet" entrepreneur, you might say. I was featured on a local *Good Morning America*-type television show, was the feature story on a local television station's five-day series called "Rags to Riches," and found myself frequently appearing both on television and radio talk shows.

My success in real estate would have been a hollow victory if I hadn't matched it with success on the home front. Luckily, I loved being a father, and I never forgot to keep my priorities straight. It paid off during those happy, progressive years with a wonderful family life.

When we first got married, I worked all the time. Then when I got into the real estate business, I worked from six in the morning until one at night for two years straight. All I did was work during that first period of our marriage. But luckily, I worked in an office at home, so I was never really "away" as we started building a family.

In fact, I was very close to my children. I wouldn't have had it any other way. You see, when I got married I wanted kids. I remember wanting kids as far back as when I was eight years old delivering newspapers. I remember promising myself way back then that I would start having kids when I was 20. And I did. That was my goal. I told myself this over and over and over again. That's what I wanted. That's what I was looking for. A lot of people get married looking for a relationship, wanting to go out partying, wanting to travel all over the world. I didn't want any of that. I wanted children.

Why? Because I love kids. It's as simple as that. Some people love skiing, dogs, whatever. I love kids. You can sit down and be genuine with a child and you'll get instant gratification because they smile back and they know when you really care about them. Adults aren't like that. They play games. They suspect that you care for some selfish reason. I get along with kids much better than I get along with adults.

It's uncanny. I can be on a plane or in a restaurant, and a little child can look me directly in the eyes, and it's like there's an immediate connection.

I remember when I taught Sunday School in the Catholic church. I made the effort to meet the parents of all the kids in the class. Normally, a Sunday School teacher would go, teach the class, and that was it. But I wanted to meet the parents to get some insights into their children. Because I really loved those kids.

When we had our first baby on July 22, 1979, I was in heaven. I thought I knew what it was to love children before, but it wasn't until we had our little Lia that I knew how high and how deep that kind of love can go.

As I said, I worked out of my home during the first

part of my real estate career, and though I worked long hours, I was right there at home for my kids. I was there for all their births. After Lia came Kevin on July 27, 1980. Jeffrey was born June 30, 1982, and Janelle followed him just after Christmas, on December 29, 1984.

All my kids rolled over for me. They all talked for me. They all walked for me. I was always there.

As our family started growing and I began working outside the home and doing very well financially, I cut my work hours down so that I only worked during the kids' school hours. I worked from 9:00 a.m. to 3:00 p.m. I'd pick them up from school, take them home, and I'd be with them. I'd take the kids out on dates each week, to a movie, bowling, miniature golfing ... whatever they wanted to do. I planned my career around them because they were the most important part of my life.

And my life, both privately and professionally, was better than I had ever dreamed possible.

The Good Life

One year I rented a limousine and a chauffeur for an entire winter. You see, my Jaguar refused to go slow. Consequently, I had two speeding tickets. If I got a third ticket, I'd lose my driver's license. Business was going at a fast pace and I was afraid that if I kept driving I would lose my license, so I rented the limo.

My success in real estate investing was responsible for many material blessings.

One of those blessings was a Jaguar. I had wanted a Jag since I was a little kid. When I built models, I'd build models of Jags. It wasn't that I wanted to go out and get the flashiest car. I just loved Jaguars. And it wasn't like I was one of these owners that lived and died over whether the car got a scratch or not. It was just a car, and I knew I could get another one.

In fact, I offered to let my friend, who drove me over to pick it up when I bought it, drive it first. He couldn't believe it. And I used to let our 16-year-old baby sitter, Margo, take it home with her overnight. *No one* could believe that!

The winter I rented a limousine and driver to avoid getting another ticket, I remember taking my kids to school. They went to a private school and their schoolmates thought it was real cool to be driven there in a limo by a chauffeur. In fact, they made up a little song that went, "Here comes Lia in the limo ..."

It was a lot of fun, but I didn't put on airs like "Here's John Ross, the hot shot real estate investor with the limousine and chauffeur." I flat out told people that I had the limo only because I didn't want to lose my driver's license, and it was less expensive than if I had gotten another ticket and had to get assigned risk insurance and all that sort of thing.

There were other symbols of success in my life at that time. I had close to $200,000 worth of credit in various credit cards alone. On two of these cards, I had $25,000 credit limits. I was never late making payments – whether paying bills or paying employees.

Although I had a nice car, and certain other "nice" things, we really didn't spend as much money as a lot of other people would have given the same opportunity. One reason is that we didn't travel. I wanted to travel. But my wife didn't. I'd come home and say, "Hey, let's go to Europe," or "Let's go to the Orient," and she'd say, "No, let's wait until the kids get older." She never wanted to leave the kids. So I figured we wouldn't be traveling for the next 18 years.

I also wanted to get out and start doing workshops around the country, but she didn't want me to get out in the world. So I didn't go anywhere.

I was making enough money during that period of my life to afford to be generous, which is something I love to be. For example, I gave my foreman a truck, a house, and a vacation to Florida.

In fact, I treated everyone who worked for me like a king or a queen. I gave them excellent pay, great vacations, and an incredible working environment. I let them pick their own holidays, sick days, and so on.

It wasn't like a job for us. It was like a family – a literal family.

If I knew someone who was having financial difficulties, I'd hire them. I hired people that weren't even skilled, and trained them. Many of them didn't know what they were doing at first. I remember having sinks that would fall through ceilings and that sort of problem. But the people eventually learned, and I made a ton of money because of it – because I didn't have to worry about anyone stealing from me. And I didn't have to worry about anyone not working.

I never, ever checked up on Rick, my foreman. I gave him total, 100 percent, exclusive control over hiring and firing, salaries, raises, and inventory. I totally trusted my people, gave them complete responsibility in their spheres, wrote them notes to tell them how much I appreciated them, and paid them very well.

They say that "what goes around comes around," and I found this to be true with my people. I treated them well, and they treated me well. They were wonderful!

When you know that somebody believes in you, I've always felt that you can't help but do your best. When somebody trusts you, appreciates you, and believes in you, it's almost like a power comes over you that forces you to do better than you've ever done before. I gave my people that kind of trust, and they lived up to it.

I only had trouble with one guy – a maintenance/construction worker. He came over to my house to fix something once and my kids didn't warm up to him. That usually says a lot about someone. Anyway, he made a sexual remark to one of my secretaries and I fired him. Everybody thought I was nuts because he was one of my best workers. They said, "Man, you didn't need to fire him. You could have just talked to him." But this guy violated my trust, and he was a reflection of me, so I fired him instantly.

I'm glad I did. I found out later that he had been taking time off during the day to sleep with a tenant in one of our buildings.

It hurt to fire him. I had treated him well. I remember before all this happened, I had overheard him talking to someone in the office one day about how his dad was dying and how he'd like to fly his sister, who lived in California, to be with him, but couldn't because of the cost. I asked him to come into my office, and when he told me the situation, I wrote him a check for $500 on the spot to fly his sister out.

You see, I had enough money to do whatever I wanted. I thought, "Hey, I've been blessed financially, and I should be doing more with this money than just satisfying myself. So I'll help people out when I can." And I did.

Things were going *so* well for us, in fact, that I began playing with the idea of going into at least a semi-retirement and moving the family to the "perfect" city. My father had died at the age of 58. My uncles had died in their 30s. I didn't intend to work myself to death and follow this family tradition.

The challenge was, we didn't know which city was the "perfect" city. We knew it wasn't Rochester. For one thing, it was too cold. So I bought a book called *The Places Rated Almanac* which asks hundreds of questions like, "Do you prefer better education over medical services?" and so on, and finally tells you which cities best match your preferences.

The book told me that four cities fit my criteria: Phoenix, Honolulu, San Diego, and Atlanta. The process of choosing one of those cities would take me two years, on and off.

I first tried Phoenix. Before actually taking time to go there, I sent out a survey to 100 Phoenix residents, selected from the telephone book. In the survey, I explained that we were interested in moving there and wanted their personal opinions regarding how they felt about their city. The response was great – over 30 percent of them responded. The survey asked questions like, "What do you like most and least about Phoenix?", and "Did you move to Phoenix from the East?" Many of the responses came back unfavorable because they missed the greenery of the East, so I crossed Phoenix off the list.

Next, I tried Honolulu. I was already scheduled to go there for a ten-day seminar. Two days after returning home from the seminar, I turned around and flew back to Honolulu to continue my investigations. After 10 more days there, I had a great tan, but couldn't see my family living there. I felt trapped being on an island.

Next, San Diego. I spent more than a month in California. I spent a lot of time in LaJolla and Mission Viejo, both just outside San Diego. There were certainly some pluses about beach communities with money oozing out of them, but the pace of life was beyond fast, and I couldn't get used to the smog.

Last stop: Atlanta. After three days in Atlanta, I knew I had found home! I felt so relaxed and peaceful there. The residents loved their city and I didn't hear a single person say he wished he lived somewhere else. The economy was good. The weather was wonderful, too.

The day I returned home, I started making plans to move my family to Atlanta and open up another office there. Many of my workers were excited – they wanted to move to Atlanta, too, and help open up that office. We were all excited about having two offices – one in Rochester, one in Atlanta.

Yes, we were living the *good life* during those halcyon days that now seem so far away. We were young, healthy, and together. We had money to live well and time to spend together. What more could anyone ask? It seemed as though my wife and I and the kids were acting out the unwritten ending of a storybook fairy tale whose last sentence reads, "And they lived happily every after...."

Funny how life can change.

The Storm After the Calm

There are three problems with sitting on top of the world. First, it's easy to lose your balance. Second, if you do fall, you have a lot further to drop. Third, when you're used to heights, normal altitudes seem very low.

I didn't know it at the time, but my first missteps – the missteps that made me lose my balance and set me up for a terrible fall – were thinking I was invincible, not getting experienced help, forgetting where I had come from, not appreciating all my blessings, and giving John T.'s son (the president of John T.'s realty company) a blanket mortgage around my 22 properties in exchange for the $250,000 line of credit.

Actually, I had pledged more than $750,000 in mortgages besides. Why? Because I was excited about our future relationship, because I trusted and liked him (I saw in him a father image), and because I wanted to raise the line of credit's limit as soon as possible. I figured that if he already had the security, it would be easy. At the time I thought it was a smart move. Boy, was I wrong!

I was paying him prime plus 2 percent interest, plus 5 percent of the sales price of the properties I bought with his line of credit. I knew that was high, but I felt it would be fine with the prices we were getting. The notes were 90-day notes, and it was my understanding that he'd work with me and "roll" the notes if I couldn't pay them back after 90 days for interest-only payments until I could.

Everything went well at first. Ninety days after the first note was taken out, I was prepared to pay the principal and the interest back, but all John T., Jr. asked for was the interest. So I went out and bought four properties for cash, so I could get a better deal. That meant I had all the principal out in properties. Then the market dropped, and the next time the note came due, he called everything due unexpectedly – both principal and interest. I couldn't sell my properties fast enough. He suggested that I let his agents sell them. The only problem with that was that they would sell them for 80 percent of what I was getting. Yes, it would be faster, but I would lose a ton of money.

I told him I would sell the properties myself, but I needed a little more time. He called the notes due anyway. He had every right to do so. But where would I find $250,000 in ten days?

I went to the banks, but kept running into dead ends. There was speculation that since John T. was the biggest real estate and mortgage broker in the city, he had a lot of influence with the banks. And of course, if I couldn't come up with the $250,000, he stood to gain over $2 million of my assets. This was nothing more than speculation, however, and I didn't want to believe it.

To make a long, sad story short, I was forced into

bankruptcy, both as a corporation and personally. All the properties were gone. All the mortgages were gone. Even some of my personal things were gone, such as my Jaguar. I could probably have kept this, but I didn't want to be driving around in a Jaguar when several investors had lost money with me. We had a quarter-million dollar house at the time, and we didn't have to move out of it since we still owed $220,000 on the mortgage.

The bankruptcy was a tremendous emotional strain. People had been serving papers on me every other day, it seemed. Every time the doorbell rang, I would think it was someone else serving papers on me and my blood pressure would skyrocket. The problems the bankruptcy caused would continue to be a source of severe stress over the next five years.

Still, even though it was a tremendous blow, I've always been a fighter. I decided to come out swinging, rebuild my fortune, and make things right with anyone who had been financially hurt by my setback.

I immediately started another company called Check Mate Realty of Rochester Corp. All my employees stayed with me. We stayed in the same office and kept the same equipment. I found two investors who came up with the money that was needed to get things going again.

I hid nothing from these investors. I told them everything, and rather than being put off by it, they seemed to appreciate my being candid, and trusted me all the more.

My plan was to go on doing real estate deals as

before, but instead of the company taking title to the properties, the investor would, and I would get paid a "finder's" fee for finding the properties, be paid for fixing them up, then get a percentage after they were sold. This actually turned out to be better than the way we did it before the bankruptcy.

All in all, things were beginning to look up again. My business was back on track. We were making money. And we were in the final stages of getting everything ready to fulfill our dream and move to Atlanta as we had planned to do before the bankruptcy.

Or so I thought.

It was July, 1988 – just three days before we were scheduled to load up our bags, say goodbye to Rochester, and head for our new home in Atlanta. I had awakened that morning excited with anticipation for the move, anxious to get to the office and tie up all the last-minute details that would need attention.

That was the morning that the two FBI agents paid a visit to my office and took me away with them. Needless to say, it was *one* last-minute detail I hadn't been counting on having to deal with....

With that final memory – still agonizingly fresh in my mind – the motion picture of my life's story came to an abrupt end, like an old movie that gets caught in the projector and melts away under the heat of the projection lamp.

By replaying my life's saga up to that dark morning, I had perhaps come to a better understanding of who I was, why I am the way I am, and why I do the things I do. But the exercise hadn't eased the pain. Nor had it altered reality.

I was still trapped in the harsh present, looking out through the cold steel bars of a dingy jail cell.

Tumbling Down the Ladder

There are people who claim to have the gift of seeing into the future. I'm glad I'm not one of them. As low as I was the day I walked out of that jail, I hadn't hit bottom. I would fall much lower in the coming few years. I thank God I couldn't peer into the future that day, or I can't say what I would have done.

I spent three days in jail, charged with ten counts of grand larceny, not knowing whether I'd be locked up for another hour, another day, another year, or the rest of my life. Needless to say, I was in shock. So was my wife. My mother, sisters, and brother couldn't believe it when they heard. Nor could my employees. They, too, were like family.

Bail was a problem. They set it at $50,000, which is higher than they set for most hardened criminals. Although my business was back on track after the bankruptcy, my financial resources still were nil. The bankruptcy had taken everything, and I had only enough cash to keep my family going.

In short, I couldn't come up with bail. I had been a millionaire, holding over $2 million worth of real estate. Now I couldn't come up with the money to get me out of jail!

Tracy went to her father for help. *He refused.* When she told me, it was like someone had twisted a knife in my gut. Until then I hadn't realized how devastated Bob must have been by my decision to leave his business, nor how bitter he was about it. His refusal to help at such a desperate time certainly drove the point home. Tracy was hurt, too. In fact, that was the last time she would speak to him for years to come.

It was my mother that put up bail. I don't know all the details, but she used her house as a form of collateral or security. Still, it took three days to get me out.

The only consolation during that three-day nightmare was the way the guards and the inmates treated me. I'm sure they could tell by the look on my face that I had never been in that situation before, and contrary to what you see in the movies, they treated me with compassion.

For instance, when you first go in, they put you in one big room. There might be 30 or 40 people in it, and you might have to spend the whole night there, like cattle. They took me out of there way ahead of my turn and put me in my own room with my own bunk.

The guards weren't rough, abrasive, or pushy with me. They looked me in the eye, and the moment they did that, their whole disposition changed in terms of how they treated me. It was obvious to them that I didn't belong there – that I was an exception to the rule.

The inmates treated me well, too. They could have ignored me and gotten tough with me, but instead they explained things to me, and basically showed me the ropes. They were very helpful. Of course, the fact that

I was so upset that I couldn't eat and gave them my food made them feel better about me, I'm sure. But that was just part of it.

I don't know what I would have done if they had treated me the way they do in the movies. Under those extremely difficult conditions, the kindness those people showed me couldn't have been more appreciated. I vowed that somehow, someday I would return the favor. (That day would come in Atlanta, about a year later.)

Ironically, the day I walked out of jail was the day we were supposed to have moved to Atlanta. It goes without saying that we didn't move that day. My wife and I were both frantically busy trying to cope with the changes precipitated by my arrest.

One of the first things I had to do was find a good criminal attorney. That's not an easy thing to do. I mean, it wasn't like I had a Rolodex full of names and telephone numbers for good trial lawyers. Some calls were made. One person we tried to contact was the president of Kodak Corporation. We had met before. We were both members of the same church.

We received a referral to the attorney I decided to use. My mother had already offered to pay for my attorney with funds from the $100,000 life insurance benefit she had received after Dad died. It was difficult for me to accept this generosity, but I had no choice. I couldn't afford an attorney myself (the final tab would be $25,000), and the cold, hard facts were that if they threw the book at me and gave me the maximum sentence on each count, I could get an 88-year sentence! I wanted to do everything in my power to avoid that possibility.

So I called the referral. He is a very successful, very wealthy criminal attorney. He said, "I don't need this case. Whether I take it or not is totally up to you." I asked him what he meant. He said, "It's up to you, depending on what *you're* like."

So we talked. I explained that a group of investors had been frightened by the Tom T. incident (the young swindler that bilked so many people in the Rochester gallery deal). These investors thought that I was too smart to go bankrupt. For some wild reason, they felt that I set up the bankruptcy on purpose. I think they had watched too much TV.

After I talked to my prospective attorney for about 15 minutes, he said that the charges were outlandish, and that he'd take my case.

As for my business, I found it emotionally impossible to go on with it. All my employees thought the charges against me were absolutely ridiculous. They were all there when I went to the office when I got out of jail. I told them it was over. They were sad because we had a good business going, and we were like family, as I said before. But they understood and did everything they could to let me know that they appreciated me and supported my decision. "You've got all this to deal with," they told me. "Don't even think of worrying about us."

Because of the bankruptcy and the way this new business had been structured (to generate cash flow, but not equity), I didn't get anything out of it when we closed the doors.

As soon as things settled down from frantic to merely hectic, we decided that it was time to go ahead with our move to Atlanta. Well before my arrest we had leased a $350,000 home there for the coming year with money my mother had loaned me, so it made sense to go since it was already paid for. (If I had known I was going to have these problems, I never would have leased such a large home, but my new business had been producing a good income that I assumed would only increase after expanding into the Atlanta area.)

Unfortunately, I personally couldn't leave New York at that time. My attorney had to first petition and convince the court that I wasn't going to run away to Atlanta and disappear. We decided that Tracy and the kids would go on ahead, with the understanding that I would follow as soon as I could.

They had been through a lot of turmoil because of my bankruptcy and arrest, and I wanted them to have as much stability in their lives as possible under the circumstances. I felt that going ahead with the move – even if I couldn't come right then – would be their best bet of getting that stability.

So they left about a week after I got out of jail. For me, being without my family made a tough situation even tougher. Some husbands and fathers would probably welcome an opportunity to take a vacation from the demands of family life. Not me. But it was best for them. I wanted to get them into a new home where they could feel secure and we could start over and build a beautiful new life.

My desire to do this was heightened by the fact

that my wife and I had been having some problems even before the bankruptcy. We had married young, and we were two very different people. Plus, the success I had experienced caused me to feel superior, and I had justified and rationalized behaviors that were wrong. It seemed that the only things we had in common were the children and our involvement in the church. So we'd been going to counselors to try to improve our relationship.

It was another three weeks until I got permission to leave New York. During that time I lived in Rochester with a wonderful family I knew from church. They had 14 kids, so I guess one more wasn't too much of a burden. I was kept busy with the attorney and tying up loose ends until I left.

A Time of Trials

When I finally arrived in Atlanta, the casual observer would have looked at the Ross family and said, "Now there's a nice, happy, upwardly mobile family with the world by the tail." How deceptive appearances can be! Instead of entering the "Promised Land" the way I originally thought I would – as a millionaire in semi-retirement – I was now broke, unemployed, and waiting with growing anxiety for my case to come to court – a case that could put me away for 88 years!

I didn't have the luxury when I finally got to Atlanta of sitting back and licking my wounds. I had to work to feed my family. But after all I'd been through, I couldn't emotionally bear getting back into real estate investments. Also, while my case was hovering over me like a black cloud, I couldn't look people in the eye and talk to them about doing a deal.

I knew I could sell, so I began scanning the newspapers in search of a company and a product to hook up with. After finding several shady companies and several very unimpressive managers, I ran into one opportunity that looked promising. It was National Safety Associates, a company that manufactured and sold water filters using direct marketing.

I had sold water filters for a brief time in my late teens and knew enough about them to realize that this was a good product. As far as income potential went, the company had a multi-level marketing program something like Amway's, so it was open-ended. I met an ex-truck driver who was selling the filters, and discovered that he was making in excess of $500,000 annually! All the lights were green, so I signed on.

I began selling water filters door-to-door, a sales technique I know well. I concentrated on selling, rather than building a multi-level organization. More than once, as I walked from house to house knocking on doors trying to get people to buy the filters, I thought how funny it would be if I met someone who had known me in New York before my life began falling apart. I could just hear it: "Hey, aren't you the self-made millionaire who gave seminars and used to be on TV all the time? I thought you were one of America's rising young business stars!"

If life is anything, it's interesting.

Although I did fairly well with NSA, I wasn't making the kind of money I had hoped to. I stayed with it, though, until my case came before the judge.

I waited *almost a year* for my case to come before the judge. Needless to say, this was an extremely difficult time for me. Although I worked hard at keeping a positive mental attitude, and although everyone I talked with told me the case would be thrown out, the idea that I *could* be facing up to an 88-year prison term (the worst-case scenario) was something I couldn't get out of my mind. It could have been the end of me! The anxiety this caused was a constant strain on me mentally, emotionally, and physically.

Meanwhile, our marriage deteriorated further. Although we lived in the same house, we became more and more estranged. It was as if there was a shroud over our home. It was such a strange sensation that I can't put it in words. It was almost as if I was out of my body watching all this take place.

It was during this same period that my mother died. Ever since Dad's passing, Mom seemed to have lost her will to live. She acted as if she had nothing to get out of bed for each morning. It is true that when people lose their will to go on living, their bodies break down and die. My mother was the perfect example of that.

Mom's death broke my heart. We had been so close. She meant so much to me, and had helped me so selflessly when I desperately needed it. And now she was gone.

My health began to worry me. The doctor said I had high blood pressure and put me on medication for it. He told me I needed to get rid of the stress in my life. What a joke!

The fact that all my former real estate holdings had fallen into disrepair and lost their values under the supervision of the bankruptcy court's appointed trustee didn't help matters. Even if the court could have sold them for half their original value, everyone would have been paid off and I would have gotten a half million dollars to start over again. But I realized now that that wouldn't happen – that about $2 million in assets had been sucked down the drain.

I felt as if I was in a downward spiral – that I was rapidly losing everything that had ever meant anything to me. During those black, black days, it was my faith in God and the intense love I felt for my children that kept me going. We had our full family by then – four beautiful, wonderful kids – and coming home to them each evening was my link to anything that even came close to happiness.

The day finally arrived when my case was scheduled to come to court. I flew back to New York. My brother and a sister and her husband came to give me moral support. I had been given the choice of having a jury trial, or letting the judge decide the case. I chose the latter option because of a show I had seen called *You Are the Jury*. In the show they had presented a case for and against a man accused of murder. Then the viewers called in to vote whether the defendant was guilty or innocent. Eighty percent of the "jury" said he was guilty. But in fact, he was innocent. I didn't want to put my life in the hands of a jury. I decided to let a judge handle it.

When my name was read, I approached the bench. It was May of 1988. Opening statements were made, the judge nodded and shook his head, and *in less than 15 minutes – after almost a year of waiting – it was over.*

The judge echoed my attorney's words when he said that the whole thing was absolutely ludicrous. He told me that my case never should have come to trial; that it never should have gotten as far as his court.

He didn't actually apologize, but his voice was apologetic. After he threw the case out, he spent some time and talked to me as a father would talk to his son, giving me personal counsel. He said that I needed to start my life over again. He counseled me to go forward without the heavy burden of bitterness and malice about what had happened. He admonished me to rebuild my life without getting caught up in crippling feelings of vengeance against the people who had unjustly accused me, and the system that had let things get as far as they did. He said these negative feelings would destroy me if I let them. He said the entire situation was incredibly unfortunate, but that I had no choice but to start over.

I was glad the judge said that. I'd like to think that I wouldn't have gotten tangled up in those negative feelings anyway, but his warning helped me watch out for them.

For my own sanity, though, I *did* look back and try to figure out why my case went as far as it did. Hindsight is 20-20 vision, they say, and in this case it was easy to look back and see what had probably happened. You see, the district attorney at the time of my arrest was just getting ready to quit his job and go into private practice. I really think that he was over-zealous about my case because it was a highly publicized one, and because he wanted all the publicity he could get in order to nail down the best private sector job he could get.

When he quit, a woman took his place. I think that she was afraid to throw this case – her spotlight case – out for fear that people would think she was "soft," or that she couldn't handle it. So she fought it even harder.

The net result was that a case that both my attorney and the judge felt was absolutely ridiculous went all the way to court. And because of it, a life – *my life* – would never be the same.

More Walls and Dead Ends

It would be nice if this were the turning point of my story; if I could say, "After my case was dropped the sun came out, the birds began to sing again, I rebuilt my life, and we lived happily ever after." That would be nice. But that's not what happened. I had lost my business, over $2 million in assets, and almost a year of my life. My father and mother were dead. I had spent time in jail. My credit was shot. And I had no money to rebuild my life. Still, I hadn't hit bottom.

Now that the court case wasn't hanging over my head, I wanted to get back into real estate investments.

But my wife was against it. She was afraid that the same sort of thing that had happened in New York might happen again. She said if I wanted to go back into real estate, that she could only handle it if I got a license and worked for a broker selling houses.

I explained that my problem wasn't real estate – it was an error I made by trusting someone who loaned me money, and signing over too many assets to him. But she didn't recognize the distinction.

As I've already mentioned, our marriage relationship was not the best even before the bankruptcy and arrest. By this time, it was all but dysfunctional. Even though being a regular real estate agent went completely against my grain, I decided to do as Tracy suggested and give it my best shot. It was an attempt to keep our marriage from falling totally apart.

I took the classes, got my real estate license, and hated every minute of it.

My first job as a real estate agent was with Remax in Norcross. The broker/owner was an excellent relocation agent, but was having trouble managing his sales people. Consequently, the office wasn't doing well. After getting to know him I became manager of the company, and he made a gentleman's agreement to give me one-third of the company.

I spent a few months trying to make the necessary changes to turn things around. Unfortunately, the sales staff didn't like the idea that I was young, 30-year-old "Yankee," and that I hadn't been a Realtor before. They resisted my ideas. They didn't like using creative ways to sell and finance properties, such as the lease-purchase program. Some negative things were said, there was a lot of contention and back-biting flying around, and I finally decided to leave the firm before I went crazy. I couldn't stand seeing people sitting around talking about their problems and complaining.

The next office I joined was another Remax office: Remax of Atlanta. This was the biggest Remax office in the country, and Lee, the owner/manager, was a true professional. But here, too, there were problems. I was considered a maverick by the other sales people because I was coming from the investment side of the business –

not the agent/sales side.

For instance, when an investor puts a contract together, it's totally different than when a Realtor puts one together. Even the wording. A Realtor will generally just use a standard contract and fill in the blanks. I would use the contract, then add on a few pages of addendums. The other agents didn't like that. And they didn't like the fact that I would buy a property and get a commission besides. It was obvious that I wasn't a "Realtor." Sure I had the license, but I wasn't one of *them.* I didn't like the way they did business, and they didn't like the way I did business. I didn't fit in.

Because of all this, Lee would get calls from agents who didn't like the way I was doing things. Then he'd have to call me in and talk to me as if I were a school boy in trouble. This didn't sit well with me. After a few months there, we decided it would be best for me to leave before the situation dragged me down further, and before Lee would have to ask me to go.

Next stop: Metro Brokers. Metro is similar to Remax, except it is a local company. Here again, I was short-lived because I stirred up the water with my investor's ways. I called the company's two owners to get names of people who worked a specific area so that I could refer a client of mine to them. I got three names. The first said he wouldn't pay me over a 20 percent referral fee, even though my client was ready to buy, the area was picked out, and the type of house was already determined.

The second agent was a woman. We set up a time to meet at my office, which was also my house. A few hours before our appointment, she called and said she didn't feel comfortable about meeting at my house. I couldn't believe her! I said there was no way I was going to go somewhere just to give her a referral. We had some unpleasant words, and the next thing I new, the owners of the company told me they heard I had made a pass at an agent, and asked me to take my license to some other brokerage.

I *really* couldn't believe this! I was disappointed in the owners for believing her, or at least for using her lie as an excuse to get rid of me, just because I didn't fit the Realtor mold. I insisted on a meeting with both the owners, and told them what I thought of them, concluding with a promise to sue them if they spread the slander. They agreed and I was off.

I was investigated *three times* by the real estate commission. Every time I wrote a contract or did a deal that didn't conform to their fill-in-the-blank mentality, someone would report me. I would then have to explain what I did, and the commission would say, "Okay." Everything I did was legal and ethical, but it was also *different*, and so I was constantly getting my knuckles rapped.

I have never been one to coast through life. I've always been ready to stir things up and change circumstances for the better when I see a need to do so. But most of these people were resistent to change. They wanted jobs, not opportunities. They felt that the way they did things was the only way, and that every other way was wrong.

The straw that broke the camel's back was what

happened to my relationship with the *Realtor* magazine in Atlanta. Ken, the editor, liked me, and I began writing articles for his publication. This made me quite visible, especially because the first article was a cover story that revealed everything that had happened to me, including the bankruptcy and the arrest by the FBI. Ken liked the article so much that he asked me to write for him on a regular basis.

The article worked against me, though. I quickly discovered that real estate agents like their industry to be noncontroversial. But *I* am extremely controversial. This didn't sit well with them.

After writing a few other articles for the magazine, Ken started getting calls from some of the other Realtors. They said, "Hey this guy isn't a Realtor – he's an investor with a license. And he's been in jail. We don't want to see any more of his articles in the magazine!"

So that was that. I learned a valuable lesson from all this: If you're trying to do something that's not "you," it's not going to work no matter where you go or how you do it. If you're a tennis player and you try to drive a bus for a living, you're eventually going to get everybody so mad at you that nobody's going to ride your bus. It's not that you're a bad person – it's just that what you're trying to do isn't what you should be doing with your life.

So much for trying to beat a round peg into a square hole. So much for politics. So much for back-stabbing and petty jealousies. It was time to be the person I was really meant to be.

And why not? Tracy was the only reason I had

forced myself to act out the part of a Realtor anyway. And she was now no longer a part of my life....

Hitting Bottom

In the Bible, there's a story about a man named Job who loses everything. He loses his possessions, his wealth, the respect of his neighbors – even his family. One day his former friends drop by. He's sitting on a dung heap, covered with boils, wearing sack cloth and ashes. Instead of comforting him, they basically say, "Tough luck, Job, but you brought it on yourself," and walk away. Some people read the Book of Job in a detached, intellectual sort of way. Not me. When I read it, it rips my heart out. Because I understand what Job went through.

During my "Realtor days," my wife and I separated. My attempt to be the kind of person she wanted me to be in business widened rather than bridged the already broad gulf between us. Like all people who are not true to their real selves, I became an angry, frustrated, bitter person during those trying months. I tried not to show it, but inwardly, I was a mess. And so was our relationship.

The situation finally became unbearable. I realized (and I think Tracy did, too) that all of us would be better off if we called it quits. Apart, we might have some chance of finding our way again. Together, we would only continue on our downward spiral.

I've spent a lot of time wondering what went wrong between us. Was it all me? Was it the money? Tracy was, and is, a good person. She is probably the best mother I've ever met. She made a pact with herself when she was young that when she got married and had kids, her kids were going to have a great mother.

So when we had kids, she gave every ounce of her energy to them. And when we joined the new church, she gave time and energy to both her kids and the church. This left about one percent of her time for me, and I need a lot of attention. Growing up, my mother paid an incredible amount of attention to me, and I had trouble dealing with getting almost no attention from my wife.

She was noble in wanting to enhance the children's lives every day. It's not like she was doing anything bad or wrong. It was just that John Ross was slowly dying. And our relationship was dying. The counselors we'd go to would tell us what was happening, but unfortunately, knowing what was happening didn't make the lack of attention and affection and the differences between us much easier for me to handle.

We never fought. I never really got mad at her. It's hard to get mad at someone who wasn't doing anything wrong and is a good person. But we were becoming more and more polarized, having less and less in common.

I finally took the initiative and left. We were still living in the same big home we had moved into when we first arrived in Atlanta. There were still three or four months left on the lease, so Tracy and the kids continued living there.

When I left, I didn't have a red cent and had nowhere to go. I took with me some clothes and one sofa so that I'd have something to sleep on. That was it.

Fortunately, I was selling some homes for an investor, and he let me to stay in one of them until it sold. I lived there on my sofa for two months.

During that time, Tracy and I got together and talked. We decided we should give our marriage one final try by going to a counselor again. We did, but it still didn't help. So we made our separation final and started the necessary proceedings, which would culminate in our legal divorce early in '89.

The separation and divorce was a painful and unfortunate thing. In fact, it was a blow I never thought I'd get over.

When the lease on our house was up, Tracy and the kids moved into a rental home for a few months. Then came the *coup de grace* – the final shot to the head: she took my four children and moved to the other side of the country, to Oregon, where she had family. Until then, I had at least been able to see them frequently. Now thousands of miles would stand between us, and I didn't have the money to fly out for an occasional visit.

Our first child, Lia, was nine years old when all this was happening. Kevin was eight. Jeffrey was six, and little Janelle was almost five. I thought I'd felt hard knocks before that day they left for Oregon, but I had experienced nothing compared to the crushing pain I experienced when I waved goodbye to them that bitter morning. It was like saying goodbye forever!

I've always had an intuitive feeling that if one part of life slaps you in the face really hard, other aspects of your life will compensate for it by going especially well. I think a lot of people have this feeling. But I guess that was just wishful thinking on my part. Losing my family was by far the hardest hit I could have taken, yet instead of compensating, other aspects of my life ganged up on me and slapped me down, too.

After I got settled in Atlanta, I went to a local correctional institution and offered to teach a real estate investing class to the inmates. This was my way of repaying the kindness that was shown me during my traumatic time in jail in New York.

This sort of thing had never been done before, and it took over a year and a couple tons of red tape to pull it off. I began teaching the first real estate workshop the prison system had ever had right around the time my divorce became final, in early '89.

I was excited. This seemed to be the one thing that was actually turning out well in my life. I found it extremely gratifying to do work inside a prison facility. The rewards of the work helped to fill the other voids in my life during that difficult time. The ten-week course was offered to the majority of the inmate population, and covered everything from the basics of real estate to the specifics of "rehabbing" properties. Sixteen inmates came to the first session. By the time I gave the final class, we had a group of 67 graduates. These people loved the course, and were moved by the fact that some-one really cared about helping them. I received letters from each one of these individuals. They touched me deeply with their sincere expressions of gratitude for the direction and opportunity I gave them.

I got caught up in the enthusiasm, and even though I wasn't getting paid a dime, I put everything I had into that course because I truly felt it could change lives. Whenever I help someone, a warm feeling comes over me and I know that what I'm doing is right. I'll never know who benefitted the most from those classes – the inmates or me.

The course was so popular among the inmates that another one was scheduled and Atlanta's Channel Two (WSB-TV) was going to do a story on it. I got every-thing ready to go, and then, just two days before the course orientation, the whole thing was suddenly can-celed.

I couldn't believe what was happening. There was absolutely no reason not to have that course, and every reason in the world to have it. Once again, I had run head-first into a brick wall of twisted politics and events beyond my control that I hadn't even seen coming. I felt as if life had slapped me in the face, and try as I might, I couldn't figure out why. It was obvious that this wasn't the time for my prison work to move ahead, but mentally, I refused to throw in the towel. One day, I vowed, I would return to the prisons to teach.

Discouragements like the cancellation of the prison course are hard to take even when you're "up." But I was down. Way down. I couldn't even get my career off the ground. A few months before teaching the prison course, I had gone back into the real estate investment business for myself. I called the company Check Mate, after my last business in Rochester.

After setting up the realty business, I needed to find a way to make money without cash or credit – neither of which I had. It occurred to me that lease-purchases offered that opportunity. Atlanta seemed to be ripe for lease-purchases. Many owners couldn't sell their homes at that time, so they were leasing them. I started going out and finding these people and working out agreements with them that if I found someone to buy their homes, I would keep the down payment (usually about $1,000 to $1,500) for a fee.

The real reason that I got so excited about the lease-purchase program, was because I felt the desperate need to do something that would make everyone involved happy. At that point in my life I just couldn't handle people being negative. After all that had happened I couldn't deal with anybody saying anything negative or feeling that I was taking advantage of them. So I needed something that wouldn't make anyone upset. That was the lease-purchase.

The business didn't go badly, but it didn't go well either. I wasn't in an emotionally healthy state. And I wasn't in a "successful" frame of mind. I still wasn't making enough money to cover previous business expenses and to meet the high monthly child support payments I was now required to make.

I was now living in another home. When I moved out of the house I was selling for an investor, I moved into another home (a mansion, actually) in Buckhead, just a mile from the governor's mansion.

This house was owned by a man who was living in another country, and was trying unsuccessfully to sell it. I found out about it through a friend of mine. When I first looked at it, it was obvious why it hadn't been sold. The grass was three feet deep, it needed landscaping, cockroaches were everywhere, and the paint was in bad shape. I took pictures of the place and sent them Federal Express to the owner, along with an explanation of why the property wasn't selling, and what needed to be done to sell it.

Apparently, I spoke his language. He gave me the listing and the job of getting the place into good condition to sell it. I asked if I could live in the house and have my office there while I did it, and he loved the idea. After all, a home that is lived in and is being taken care of looks and smells much more marketable than an empty one.

Selling a home that size in the Atlanta area is not an easy task. The market was very soft at that price level. In addition to whipping the grounds and the home itself into shape, I placed ads in the newspapers every week, sent flyers out to agents, put signs up, held open houses, installed a brochure box in front of the property, and did everything else I could think of. Still, even though I had some good prospects, the house did not sell.

This was good for me, in a way, because the owner continued to allow me to live there. In another way, I could have used the $40,000 commission.

While struggling to get my new business up and running, I received yet another slap in the face. When I got divorced, I didn't have any money for an attorney. The result of this was that I was at the mercy of my ex-wife and her attorney, and I ended up having to pay *$5,000 a month in support payments.* I should have fought it, but I was so emotionally distraught that I would have agreed to anything. Which I did. I felt like I was the lowest life in the world. I was totally drained, so I said yes to anything they wanted.

Of course, I couldn't pay the $5,000 a month. I tried. I wanted to. But I simply couldn't. That's a ridiculous amount of money each month – especially when you have nothing. I loved my children dearly, but I just wasn't able to produce that kind of money that quickly. So I had to wait around until my ex-wife and her attorney had me arrested. And eventually that's what happened.

They put me in jail for three days. This seemed particularly cruel, since she knew how devastating that would be to me.

That was it! I had taken all I could take. I was at my breaking point. There I was, in jail for the second time in my life. I was no criminal! I was no cheat! I was just doing the best I could, trying to get along in a world that seemed to be getting a kick out of knocking me down every time I tried to stand up long enough to get my balance.

Within just the past few years, I had ridden the roller coaster of fortune from the highest peak to the lowest valley. I had lost my business, my multimillion dollar fortune, my credit, both my parents, my wife, and – most devastating of all – my four children. I had gone through the horrors of bankruptcy, had been ostracized by the local Realtor community, had been in and out of real estate sales jobs, and had been thrown in jail not once but twice. I was completely alone. I had nothing I could call my own – not even the house I lived in. There were times late at night that I would sit and look at the pictures of my children and sob.

Still, I could not give up. I could not and would not lose my faith in God and in myself. Somewhere down deep in what felt like a bottomless despair, there was a small, hard, indestructible kernel of hope.

It was all I had. But somehow it kept me going.

Bouncing Back From Despair

Someone once told me, "Nothing lasts forever. The wheel turns. The tide changes." When I finally hit bottom – not knowing at the time whether that was really the bottom, or if I had further to plunge – I took comfort in that thought. I was so low, my emotions were so brutalized, that it would have been easy to have slipped into a life of drugs, alcohol, or crime. But I kept telling myself, "This won't last forever. This can't last forever. Hang in there! The tide will turn!" And finally, it did.

When my support payment case came before the judge (luckily it didn't take a year this time!), and he found out that I had been thrown in jail for not being able to pay $5,000 monthly support payments, he went crazy! He was furious at my ex-wife's attorney for getting me to sign something that said I had to pay so much support.

In fact, the judge was so outraged that he lectured the attorney right there in public for 15 minutes. He said, "Movie stars don't even pay this kind of money! I don't know how you could have possibly imagined that this man could pay that kind of money to your client!"

He reduced my support payments to $1,500 a

month.

Looking back, I think that was the turning point – the moment when the tide began to come back in for me. It wasn't that the support payment reduction was an earth-shattering "break." Actually, it was just fair, and would still be hard to afford. But in some strange way, it gave me a feeling that things would begin moving in a positive direction in my life again. Sure, I knew I would continue to have problems and struggles; I knew that finances would continue to be a hardship; but I also had a feeling that the negative things that were happening to me would begin to decrease in proportion to the positive things that would be coming my way.

It was a question of momentum. I was due for a few good wins, for a couple of home runs. I felt it inside. And I was right. My first big win was just around the corner.

It was Halloween night, 1989. I had been invited to a Halloween party at Rupert's night club in Atlanta. At first, I didn't want to go. Being single again, I had gone through the typical "meat market" dating routine and had given up, vowing that I would not bother with women until I was wealthy again. I thought there was no reason to look, anyway. I hadn't found anyone who even held my attention, let alone who made me want to remarry. But I loved to dance. It helped me deal with stress. So I dressed up as one of the Blues Brothers – dark glasses and all – and went.

I was out on the floor dancing with a friend of mine when I turned and saw something that I first thought must be a vision. There, across the dance floor, was a female Blues Brother – dark glasses and all. She looked like my clone, except that she was smaller and feminine, even with a man's suit on. She was really enjoying her dancing, so carefree and uninhibited!

I asked my friend to excuse me for a moment and walked over to the vision. I think I wanted to touch her to make sure she was real. When I got there, all I could say was, "You dance phenomenally!"

She smiled and said that she had been watching me too, and thought the same of me. Energy was charging through my body by now like bolts of lightning. With our hats and sunglasses on, we really couldn't even see what the other person looked like. But I had a strong feeling that she was feeling the same thing I was: some sort of invisible connection between us. It was powerful!

I went back to my friend and began dancing again, but I couldn't take my eyes off my twin Blues Brother across the dance floor. When my friend went to the ladies room, I stood at the top of the stairs and just watched my vision dance. I could feel my smile getting bigger and bigger as I stared at her. The man she was dancing with stepped back so I could see her better. It was a nice thing to do. (Or maybe I just looked dangerous that night.)

I was watching her intently without even trying to hide it or be "cool" about it. I couldn't help myself. After the song ended, she walked straight across the dance floor, up the stairs, and came to a stop right in front of me. She looked straight at me without smiling, her face only inches from mine. Just when I was wondering if she was going to slap me for staring at her so blatantly, she put out her hand to give me "five," and her face – even under the glasses – broke out into the most radiant smile I had ever seen.

If I had been entranced by her dancing, I was enslaved by her smile and the touch of her hand. I told her I had to dance with her soon. I said it with the same emotion people say they have to have a drink of water when they're dying of thirst.

In the few minutes that we talked, I must have asked her six or seven times if she would go out on a dance date with me. But at the same time, I also told her that I couldn't afford to get into a relationship at that point in my life – that my focus was (and *had* to be) my business. I made that clear to her. "All I want to find is a good dance partner," I told her. She responded quickly by saying, "Well, I'm real nice, too."

I didn't do the typical thing and ask for her number. I didn't want anything about our introduction to be typical. And I didn't want to push her. So I gave her my card and asked her to call me when she could. She said she'd call the next day before noon, and told me her name was Kelly.

I was thrilled out of my mind. As she walked away, I knew I would have to leave the party and go home. I no longer could be with anyone else but her.

The next day at the office, everyone knew I had met someone very special the night before. I was excited, nervous, like a teenager waiting for his date with the prom queen.

I waited anxiously for Kelly's call. Noon came, and she hadn't called. One o'clock came, and she hadn't called. My nerves were beginning to unravel. Then, at half past one, she called. We talked feverishly for a half hour, and set up a phone date for that night.

We spent two or three hours that night on the phone together, and about the same amount of time the next night. We talked freely about everything – our lives, our dreams, our jobs, our sorrows – and were reluctant to hang up.

We had become intrigued by one another at the Halloween party. But we fell in love over the phone. And we still weren't sure what the other looked like out of costume!

After the second night on the phone, we decided to meet early the next morning at a little restaurant for breakfast. I arrived a little early. When Kelly came in and sat across the table from me and we finally really saw each other, neither of us could talk. She was beautiful! Tears filled our eyes and rolled down our faces. It wasn't just that we were physically attracted to each other, as we had hoped to be. It was more. Much more. Strange as this may sound, it was as if we had been very close before this life, and had finally found each other once again. It was a feeling of being "home at last!"

From that day on, we saw each other every day. I told Kelly *everything* about my past after our second date – the bankruptcy, the arrest, the divorce, and my four children. In comparison, Kelly had led a fairly uncomplicated single life for 28 years, so this news came as quite a shock. She cried out loud that day when she understood the difficult realities of my life – realities that had now become a part of her life, as well. Although this seemed to cast a slight shadow over our "fairy tale" beginnings, Kelly's feelings for me did not waiver. The bond we'd found together grew stronger in spite of the initial adversities we experienced.

About three weeks after we first met was Thanksgiving, and we flew to Dallas so I could meet Kelly's family. Every Thanksgiving her family goes out to their friends' land in the country about an hour and a half away from Dallas for a "Pilgrim's Thanksgiving." They have about 200 acres of beautiful, wooded property. Everybody brings a favorite dish, they have a prayer, they read a poem, and then they have Thanksgiving dinner. They take motorcycles, Jeeps, and four-wheelers along to ride around and have a good time after dinner.

I saw a side of Kelly that day that I didn't know existed. I was out on a four-wheeler looking for her, thinking she had gone out for a little walk, when I heard a motorcycle come screaming up a hill. I turned to look, and there, flying up over the rise was a wild woman on a motorcycle. It was Kelly!

I had only known her three weeks, and I had come to think of her as a dainty little woman. But there she was riding a "muscle bike" like a pro. It didn't take me long to find out that Kelly does *a lot* of athletic and outdoor things like a pro. She was her parents' first child, and her dad taught her what fathers normally teach their sons, from sports to riding motorcycles.

It was a fun day, and when it was over we went to stay with Kelly's parents for the next four or five days, which was three or four days longer than we should have stayed for my first visit! We should have exposed them to me in a smaller dosage at first. Kelly had told me before we went to just be myself. That was like letting a hurricane loose in a china shop. Her parents are calm, laid-back people, and I'm basically a whirlwind. Her mother is a designer and an educator, and her father, among other things, manages and plays the trombone in the Dallas opera. Kelly says that I sort of blasted through their house. I guess what I'm trying to say is that they didn't take to me very well initially. There were definite personality clashes.

To make matters worse, I think her parents knew right off the bat that Kelly felt I was that "right" person for her, and that nothing they could do or say would change that. She being their first child and only girl, it must have been quite a shock to them to realize that they were, in effect, giving her up to some guy they didn't know anything about except that he was a tornado of energy.

It was not an oversight on our parts that they didn't know much about me. Kelly's plan had been to bring me to Dallas, spend a wonderful Thanksgiving holiday with her family, and then, after they had fallen in love with me, she would tell them all about my past – my divorce, my kids, my arrests, my business problems ... everything.

But they *didn't* fall in love with me. So she was afraid to tell them. It would have just made matters worse at that point ... or so she thought.

After our Thanksgiving visit, we returned to Atlanta, where our relationship just kept getting better. Then

Christmas came, and Kelly went home alone to Dallas to be with her family for the holidays. Her parents spent a lot of time trying to persuade her not to marry me. They felt very strongly about it, and let her know.

My children, who were living in Oregon, were able to come to Atlanta to be with me for Christmas. I wanted Kelly to meet them before they left. When she returned from Dallas, she was already stressed out because of her parents' disapproval, and it didn't help to have me pick her up at the airport and bring her right to my home and meet my four kids! I had them all waiting for her upstairs, and had Kelly sit on the couch downstairs. Then I sent my kids downstairs, one by one, to meet her and spend a little time talking to her. She told me afterwards how nervous she had been.

She was a hit, though! The kids stayed with me for another week, and whenever we sat down to eat, they wanted to sit by Kelly. Whenever we went in the car, the wanted to sit next to her. They fought over who got to be next to her wherever we went. It worked out perfectly.

I asked Kelly to marry me on January the 18th, the night before her birthday. We had already talked about getting engaged and married, but we hadn't talked about when. It took Kelly totally by surprise, and I'll admit, it wasn't the easiest thing I've ever done. We were at my house. I said I had to tell her something important, and sat her down on the couch. I was extremely tense. So was Kelly. In fact, she told me later that she was scared to death. She thought I was going to tell her that something horrible had happened, or that I was going to drop some kind of a bomb on her. She could feel my heart racing, because I was kneeling down by her with my chest against her knee. I looked at her and tried to say something romantic and memorable a couple of times, but couldn't, and looked away. She finally said, "John, whatever it is, it's okay. You can tell me."

I was too rattled to say anything memorable after a few more attempts, so I finally just handed her the engagement ring and asked her if she'd marry me.

She was caught completely by surprise. She didn't say anything! Seconds turned to minutes, then to hours, then to days. Whole eternities flew by. (She maintains it was only about 20 seconds.) I wasn't worried – I was plain scared. I wasn't scared when the FBI agents came to get me, but I was definitely scared sitting there waiting for her to say something. It was so right, I just didn't want anything to go wrong. Finally she said yes and I could see that she was still surprised ... but very happy.

When Kelly told her parents about our engagement, they did something I'll always admire them for: they decided that they'd better try to change their attitude toward me. As truly loving parents, they were willing to forego their own feelings for the feelings of their child. I think they also realized at that point that they would either start enjoying this part of their only daughter's life, or they'd miss out on it completely.

Kelly didn't actually tell them everything about my life history until after we were married. By then they were relieved by the information, because they are perceptive people, and had felt that there were some undisclosed details that were missing from my personal history. Without having the information to fill in gaps in my life, they naturally imagined the worst. In fact, they later told me that they even wondered if I was a mass murderer or something like that!

Her mother was most upset by the fact that Kelly hadn't told her anything before then. Kelly learned a valuable lesson from this experience: to always confront and face the truth of your situation head on.

After that, Kelly's family accepted me and everything was fine. Now, they love me and treat me like their own son. They're wonderful people. We have a great relationship.

We wanted to have an April wedding in Dallas. That meant we only had three months to get everything together. Kelly's parents did more than their share of the work because they were there and we weren't. The distance created some interesting challenges. For instance, Kelly's mom found two beautiful wedding dresses at an apparel mart that were going to be sold at the end of the show at incredible discounts. She tried on the dresses herself (she says she got some interesting looks!), went and got her camera, took pictures of the dresses, had them developed quickly, and faxed them to Kelly at work so she could decide if she wanted one of them. She did. Her mom bought one of the dresses as the mart was closing. Kelly finally tried it on a few months later, and it was perfect.

Kelly and I were married on April 28th, 1990, in a little church in Dallas. When I think of what that day has meant to me, I would have to say that it was the most important and fortunate day of my life. Kelly is everything I hoped she would be, and more. Our relationship is everything I have dreamed of, and more. Kelly is my companion, my friend, and my partner in a romantic adventure that is ever-renewing, and endlessly joyful. She is an angel who was sent to be by my side and help me become the best I can be.

Our honeymoon was a dream. Although we didn't have much money at that time of our lives, a friend of mine in the travel industry got us a great deal on a trip to Puerto Vallarta, Mexico. Kelly had grown up in Texas, just across the border from Mexico, but I, being from Pennsylvania, had never been to Mexico before. We fell in love with the country, its people, and their easy-going ways. We vowed to go back regularly – a vow we have kept.

Our married life together had happy but humble beginnings. As I said, we didn't have much money. But I didn't mind. I realized that although I wanted to have money so that we could do the things we wanted to do, and achieve the dreams we had for our future, I didn't have to depend on it for my happiness. The woman of my dreams was now my reality. Somehow, I knew that my life had truly changed direction.

Back on Top Again

One good thing about being on the bottom is that when (and if) you make it back to the top, you don't take a minute of it for granted. A tall, cold glass of water is heaven to someone who just crawled out of the desert. But to someone who has never been thirsty, it's just a glass of water.

They say that good luck, like bad luck, rarely travels alone. I can vouch for that.

About the same time I met Kelly, I got a call from the *Financial Freedom Report*, a national monthly magazine for real estate investors. They wanted to do a feature article about me. I was flattered, and jumped at the chance to be featured in this magazine. I was also excited because I was still struggling with my business and finances (I had to pay my ex-wife each month, my own expenses, and the business's expenses, including the salaries of a few administrative people), and I knew that this article would give me exposure and credibility exactly where I wanted it: among other real estate investors and entrepreneurs.

You see, even though we tried to focus on lease-purchases, Check Mate was still a real estate company, I still had my real estate license, and we still did things that Realtors do just to generate income. But it wasn't working out the way I wanted it to.

For starters, I had tried to make sales people out of my administrative staff, and that simply didn't work. In addition, I do better when I can focus on one thing, and trying to keep the realty and the lease-purchase sides of the business going at the same time scattered and diluted my energies.

Also, the Realtor community and the real estate commission were a constant thorn in my side. They still called me on the carpet if I did anything out of the ordinary. This was blocking my progress. I wanted desperately to throw my license in their faces and tell them I wasn't going to play their games anymore; that I wasn't even going to be playing in the same ball park anymore.

I wanted to completely disassociate myself with the traditional Realtor involvement in real estate, and get back strictly into investing, where the real deals and the real money are made. But until I was stronger financially and had more going to sustain me in non-Realtor-oriented activities, I didn't feel that I could turn in my license.

My story was published in the April 1990 issue of the *Financial Freedom Report* – the same month Kelly and I were married! The response to that article not only verified my feelings about the direction I should take my career, but also helped me move in that direction.

The article outlined my personal story, and gave an introduction to my real estate program. Many readers were excited about the opportunity this investment technique offered and began to ask questions.

One reader called me and asked if I could spend a few days with him, teaching him my program from top to bottom, and helping him get started in real estate. I said sure, and we arranged for a consultation fee to be paid for my time and expertise.

When this happened, a bell went off in my head. For a long time, the idea had been fermenting in the back of my mind that I could do well as a consultant, helping people become successful using my ideas. After all, I had done about 500 real estate transactions. I knew them inside and out. But I hadn't really pursued offering my experience and expertise as a consultant.

Now, the opportunity was literally pounding my door down. I quickly sent out a mailing to a portion of the magazine subscribers, using the article as an introduction, and explaining that I was offering my services as a consultant who would go anywhere and spend as long as necessary with an investor in a one-on-one, on-the-job-training experience. My fee would vary, depending on how long I stayed with them and what I did with them.

After the first consulting job, the mailing created another job, then another, and so on. One day I woke up and realized that I had completely phased into the consulting business. And it was exactly where I wanted to be.

This enabled me to fulfill my dream of relinquishing my real estate license. I phased out Check Mate and created a new and exciting business entity: The Mentor Group, Inc. With this company, I would continue doing investments for myself, but primarily I would teach others, as a consultant, how to create lasting prosperity in the field of real estate. The company's name was derived from the fact that several of my consulting clients had begun to refer to me as their mentor.

During my time with these clients (who also become my friends, and often my future associates on other investments), I not only teach them the ropes, but I actually walk through the process with them, so that by the time I leave they are ready to move forward and execute actual deals that will provide them with an income and serve as a springboard to financial liberation. To my knowledge, I'm the only one who does this type of one-on-one consulting. Everyone else just sells books and tapes.

The consulting side of the business is great because I love people, and I love to help them. When I go to work with someone, and they later call me up to tell me how excited they are because their lives have changed, I feel wonderful! It's so much better than just fixing a property up, turning it around, and making a profit for yourself without really helping anyone else.

The feature article wasn't the only good thing that happened to my business in 1990. Kelly also happened! How could I have known when I first met her that this beautiful, fun-loving, charming woman would turn out to be not only my wife, but an extremely talented business partner.

It took awhile for me to coax her to step into the business partner role, however. After we got married, she continued to work in the same job she had before.

She was working for a software company, traveling around and training their customers to use their product. To me, it was obvious how valuable she could be to my business, so I started working on her immediately to join forces with me and become my partner. This turned out to be a two-stage process.

The first stage was her conversion from being an employee of a software company to being a self-employed entrepreneur. It took about four months, during which time I helped her develop a plan and make the mental adjustment necessary to quit her job and start her own business doing basically what she had been doing as an employee. She equated security with receiving a regular employee's paycheck, which of course it isn't. She had always worked for a company, and had never been out on her own in business, so it wasn't an easy step to take. This was a perfect opportunity for me to help Kelly by exercising my mentoring skills and expertise right in my own backyard! I knew she could do it, and she did.

It took courage to take the leap. Kelly said it was like letting go of one trapeze and not knowing whether the other one was going to be there for her to catch. Luckily it was, and she swung into a software training business that did very well for her. She started making as much money working a few days a week on her own as she did working full time as an employee. In fact, it could have been a profitable long-term business, but it was time for "stage two."

After having her own business for about six months, I persuaded Kelly to put it aside and be my full-time partner. During those six months, since she only had to put a few days a week into her own work, she had been helping me build The Mentor Group. I was convinced more than ever that my business needed her. Now that she felt confident in her abilities as an entrepreneur and comfortable with not getting regular paychecks from an employer, she agreed with me that it would be great for us to work together.

It turned out to be *more* than great – it was incredible. Now that we were partners, we traveled everywhere together. And we were on the road a lot. This fulfilled my life-long desire to travel, and added the exciting twist of going with someone I loved. We had already done some business traveling together. Kelly's work, both before and after she had gone out on her own, had involved traveling to her clients' offices in different cities to train them, so we always tried to coordinate our itineraries so we could travel together. Sometimes it didn't work out. Now it was a sure thing. It was wonderful to explore new places together, and build our future while we were doing it.

We got rid of the two cars we had between us and bought one car – a four-door Saab – which we used to drive all over the country while we were trying to economize. We put 40,000 miles on that car the first year. We had a laptop computer with an attachment that plugged into the car's lighter so we could work while we drove. We got a lot of our marketing work and writing done that way. Also, we listened to many, many educational and motivational tapes as we drove. Kelly even taught me to have a real appreciation for music by playing a lot of modern and classical music during our trips.

Those were great times. We had a lot of fun. The only drawback was that in the beginning it was torturous to drive so much. One of us would drive for hours and hours until we were exhausted, and then we'd switch and let the other one drive. On one trip we stayed with some of Kelly's relatives in Washington – an energetic married couple in their 60s that spent a lot of time traveling all over the country. They suggested that we switch drivers every 100 miles, which worked out to be about every hour and a half.

We tried it, and it turned out to be a phenomenally good system. We found that we could travel 600, 800, even 1,000 miles a day without getting tired as long as we switched every 100 miles. And it made it a lot more fun.

We had many unique experiences as we traveled around consulting. I worked with people shoulder to shoulder in their homes or offices for one or two or three days, and I never knew what to expect. Before I'd get there I didn't know who they were, *what* they were, what their living conditions were, or anything. I worked with one guy for a few days out of his home, which happened to be a recreational vehicle – like a Winnebago. He didn't even have a Social Security number. He kept all of his money in cash, and he had gold buried in the ground all around his mobile home!

Another guy who hired me as a consultant told us that he wanted us to stay with him because he had a nice house on the beach, and we could go waterskiing and boating, and sit out at night and watch the sunset. He said all his children would be gone, so it would be just him, his wife, Kelly, and me. He said there was a guest bedroom for us, and that there was plenty of room. From the picture he painted, we got this image of staying in a beautiful home in a resort area, going out jet-skiing after work ... the perfect work/vacation.

Although it's our rule never to actually stay at the homes of our consulting clients (we stay at hotels instead), we decided to make an exception this one time. It sounded too good to pass up.

As we drove closer and closer to this place, the value of the homes started to drop significantly. We went from a nice suburban neighborhood to a poverty-stricken area, and then on to where we were finally driving along dirt roads through what I can only describe as a dump, or maybe a hang-out for destitute hippies. We found the house, except it wasn't really a house – it was a trailer near a lake.

When we got out of the car it was raining, and there was about four inches of mud on the dirt road. We had to take our shoes and socks off to get to the trailer. When we stepped in, we saw that it was like a closet. And it wasn't empty! It was him, his wife, his wife's two daughters, both of their kids, and her son. One daughter was trying to get away from her boyfriend, who beat her. Another daughter had a habit of attacking her mother and father in the middle of the night because she was freaking out on drugs or something.... And this was where we were going to stay!

Kelly and I were laying there that night, face up in

their little bedroom, door locked, looking up at the ceiling, and we said to each other, "Let's give this guy the money back that he paid to get us here, and get out while we can!" But then we decided that our client needed someone to believe in him, and that he needed our help and our program. It would have only been worse for him if we had decided to withdraw and abandon him at that point. So we stayed, and I think we really helped. But it was difficult.

Although life on the road was exciting, interesting, and usually a lot of fun, it was also bizarre. Definitely bizarre. We would often drive to speak to groups that met in churches, schools, or meeting halls, so we'd have to change from our casual driving clothes into our dressy clothes in a McDonalds or Wendy's or some public rest room. We'd walk into the rest rooms in grubs, and a few minutes later I'd walk out in my suit and then Kelly would emerge in a nice dress looking like a million dollars.

We lived out of our car, and out of hotels. We'd eat out all the time. We'd have fast food on the road. We spent much more time in public rest rooms than either of us would care to remember. This was a particularly negative aspect for Kelly, being a woman.

We'd be gone for two or three weeks in a row, and come home for anywhere from a few hours to a day or two, take stuff out of our suitcases, put new stuff in, and take off again. It was crazy. And it was a lot of work. We got to see the country, but we sometimes felt like aliens, like homeless nomads.

Not long after I had gotten into one-on-one consulting, I had decided to take the steps necessary to expand my business to reach a broader segment of the population. It hit me one day that a lot of people who would like to benefit and learn from my real estate experience or get involved in lease-purchasing couldn't afford to pay the expensive consulting fees in order to buy my time and bring me to their city on a one-on-one basis. I began to think of how I could give these people the knowledge and skills they needed to become successful real estate entrepreneurs and lease-purchasers at a price that would fit their budgets.

The solution was obvious: we wrote and published a workbook home-study program that would teach them everything they needed to know – from A to Z – right down to the dialogues they would use when making phone calls. This course is now entitled *Lease-Purchase Profits*, and it's currently in its fifth printing. Each printing has been revised and improved.

I also contacted a writer to help me put together a book on my life story. – this book. I wanted it to serve as an introduction to me, and hopefully, as a source of inspiration to readers as they struggle with their own problems and challenges.

The workbook/tape course and autobiography were ready just in time. I had begun to find myself once again in the limelight.

Kelly and I spent much of 1991 on the national speaking tour, keeping up with the growing numbers of invitations I was receiving from some of the nation's top real estate, business, and motivational seminar groups. This gave me and our lease-purchase course nation-wide exposure. I also did quite a bit of speaking to professional groups and investment clubs, and donated quite a bit of my time to speak to young people in high schools and groups such as Future Business Leaders of America about positive thinking, starting a business, becoming an entrepreneur, and that sort of thing.

Everyone seemed to want to hear about our work and our programs. The word got around real fast that we didn't use sales hype to showcase our information. We simply explained it. A lot of real estate "gurus" were out there trying to sell their materials by saying they were easy and would make you rich quick. They were even throwing in trips to Hawaii and other "slick" promotional gimmicks.

We didn't do any of that. We didn't say our program was easy. We didn't say it would make them overnight millionaires. We didn't offer gimmicky ploys. Yet we were able to make the same percentages of sales that the other guys were making by using all the crazy claims and attractive offers. The difference was that we reached a percentage of people who were more genuine and level-headed. People told us that they appreciated and were attracted by my down-to-earth, straightforward presentations.

Business boomed. A lot of people were buying our lease-purchase home-study course at seminars, and more and more individuals wanted to participate in one-on-one consulting time with me.

About the time Kelly and I celebrated our first anniversary, the house we had been living in finally sold, and we moved into another home. We lived in one bedroom in the new house, and filled the rest of the house with office equipment and employees. That was okay because we were traveling almost all the time anyway – about 28 days out of the month – and even when we were there, we were working.

Our income was rising quickly, but we were putting it all back into The Mentor Group – into equipment, into traveling, into creating our programs and materials ... and especially into our people, so that we would have the high-quality management, marketing, and follow-up we needed. We wanted to hire the best people, because we knew that having the right people is the key to making a company grow.

Kelly and I decided that we'd rather have good people in our office than money in our pockets and a lot of glitzy material things. We spent very little of the money we made on ourselves. While our increasingly busy schedule forced us to fly more than we had done during the previous year, we still drove wherever and whenever we could.

That same year – 1991 – *Success* magazine selected me to be one of the recipients of its annual "Great Comebacks" awards. I was chosen because I had gone from being very successful, to being penniless, with virtually nothing, and then had climbed upward again to new heights of financial and professional success – all within just a few years' time. My story and photographs were featured in their August issue. Not surprisingly, exposure in a magazine of that stature gave our thriving business yet another boost. But it did even more than that for me on a personal level. It was like a final confirmation that my life was on a solid upward course.

Success From the Inside Out

As we traveled around the country teaching people how to make money and succeed in real estate and in business, it became painfully apparent to me that if people don't have their personal lives in order, they're not going to find lasting, meaningful success no matter what they do or how hard they try.

Most of my clients seemed to be trying to get rich quick. They had short-term thinking instead of long-term thinking. They were concentrating so hard on trying to make money that their personal lives were a mess. They didn't have their perspectives right. One client, for example, was smoking two packs of cigarettes a day, and was in a destructive relationship. He knew that he needed to take care of those things, but he pretended that nothing was wrong, and didn't do anything about it.

That's why I always work with our one-on-one consulting clients at the personal and family level, in addition to teaching them business principles and techniques.

It finally hit me that we should put all these "life assistance" principles and suggestions into a manual, and give it to our clients as a personal development supplement to *Lease-Purchase Profits*. Kelly played a major role in putting this project together. The manual was finished and ready to go just as we were getting ready to jump into 1992.

We gave this personal development program and manual the title *Unlock!* The title refers to "unlocking" people to reach their full potential, their ultimate business success, their true happiness, or whatever else it is they want to be or do. It has turned out to be a tremendously successful and meaningful part of what we offer, both as a product and as a part of our one-on-one consulting curriculum.

One of the things we suggest to people in the manual is that those who want to improve their lives should try changing their appearance. If someone who has been making $25,000 for years will do something to change his appearance – get a different haircut, shave his moustache, get new clothes – he's going to look into the mirror and see somebody who is different than the same old $25,000-a-year person. This technique helps people consciously and subconsciously accept the fact that they have the potential to change their lives – to earn more money, to become a different person.

There's another technique called the "mirror test" that we teach people to do in the *Unlock!* course. We tell them to look at themselves in the mirror – right in the eye – when nobody's around, and ask themselves, "What *am* I doing that I *shouldn't* be doing; and what am I *not* doing that I *should* be doing?" Then they make a list of those things, using their own criteria – not their parents' or their religions' or other people's.

We tell them that if they start to work on that list,

even if it's just a slow, point-by-point process, that they will increase their confidence, which will increase their self-esteem, which will increase their income, because people have to have confidence in the person they're dealing with in order to do business with them. We've found that as these people start to live their lives the right way, and get on track, things start falling in place for them.

As we taught *Unlock!* to individuals and groups around the country, and as people began to put its teachings to work in their lives, we were overwhelmed by the power these principles and techniques have to transform lives. The *Unlock!* program, which was coupled with our lease-purchase program, became an increasingly important part of our business, and personally, for both Kelly and I, it quickly became our favorite focus. In fact, on many occasions I have presented *Unlock!* without the lease-purchase program, because not everyone is interested in making money in real estate, yet *Unlock!* has something for everyone. Everyone can use some personal improvement.

Because of the *Unlock!* program, I was finally able to get my prison workshops again and get back inside those walls ... as a volunteer and a visitor. I've already mentioned that my own experience behind bars – brief as it was – gave me a gut-level desire to help inmates, which I consider to be the "forgotten people" of our society. The real estate investing course I taught early in '89 in one of Atlanta's correctional facilities showed me that there are many, many inmates who are desperate and thirsting for help. The people who took that course were sincerely looking for the motivation and skills needed to turn their lives around. With the *Unlock!* program, I knew I had what they had been searching for.

Logistics have been easy. We take the time to make some arrangements with the various state and federal prisons to give presentations wherever our regular speaking and consulting work takes us – from California to Florida. This has became one of my personal passions. I enjoy doing it today even more than when I started. I speak at a prison every other week or so. I spend an hour and a half with the inmates, and usually between 10 and 20 percent of the prison population attends – as many as 250 or so. These are the ones that really want to make a change.

Speaking to inmates has put us back on television: on several news programs and local talk shows. We've also been the guest on various radio talk shows for our prison program, as well as for the lease-purchase program. While all this has been nice, and has helped promote our prison work, the real pay-off has been, and will always be, the letters we get from the inmates. We have hundreds of them.

One guy really jerked my heart strings when he wrote, "... maybe if the system would have had seminars like yours before, I might not have returned to prison.... I hope that with your help I won't return here again." Another inmate wrote to his warden about my presentation, and said, "... he's the one guy who might be able to get my head in the right direction." Another gentleman wrote his warden and said that my program was "just the shot in the arm that some of us need ... not only to 'hold our heads up high' once again – but to help develop an attitude that will assure we make this our last trip to prison."   One prisoner pretty much summed up what we're trying to do when he wrote, "You may be permanently altering the paths our lives are taking, and benefit society as a whole."

I think one of the reasons why the inmates listen to me is that I'm coming in from the outside; I'm not paid by the institution; I could have ended up in their situation, but didn't; and I'm coming back to try to help the guys that unfortunately ended up there, and give them hope, but give it to them straight. I also try to make the point that they have something most of us on the outside don't: a ton of time – time to work on themselves personally, and get their heads in the right place, so that when they get out of there, their thinking will be different and they'll be able to make something of themselves.

The prison officials have given us positive feedback about our program, too. Harry L. Reynolds, Supervisor of Education for the Federal Bureau of Prisons wrote and said, "It's not often that we as correctional staff have the privilege of observing a presentation having such a profound effect on our inmates. Thank you for your truly significant contribution of great meaning to a great many people."

We've even had positive feedback from Washington.   United States Senator Sam Nunn wrote us and said, "I am most impressed with your program and with your willingness to share your experiences with those who can benefit most from them."

My passion for helping inmates turned into a crusade not long ago when Kelly and I founded The Inside Corporation, a nonprofit organization dedicated to top-quality prison self-improvement programs for inmate populations, both adults and juveniles. Our mission statement explains that The Inside Corporation exists "to enhance public safety through educational programs, activities, and support directed toward selected populations within, related to, or affected by the criminal justice system."

The sad fact of the matter is that most offenders turn back to crime within one year of their release from prison. We want to break that cycle. Somebody has to! The *Unlock!* program is our key tool in this crusade. We also have what we call *Street Link*. It's a post-release support program that provides ongoing motivational and personal development training, in group and one-on-one sessions. *Job Net* is another aspect of this whole effort. This is an ongoing support program that offers vocational and job skill training, career planning, and job networking. All these things are designed to give the inmate a new chance to turn his life around.

We funded the program pretty much by ourselves until it grew to the point that we couldn't do it alone. Recently, we've been going after funding from individuals and corporations in the private sector, and foundations of all types. All the money that comes in goes out to pay for the programs. We're also looking for other people that are willing to support our prison program with their time and talents.

We feel strongly about the importance of The

Inside Corporation. It's not only important to the inmates in this country, which now number close to 900,000, but to our society as a whole. Face it – the prison program affects *everybody*. Everybody locks their doors. Everybody worries about having things stolen. Everybody walks around in fear of being a victim of a violent crime. Every home owner pays for insurance. More and more people are buying alarm systems for their homes and cars. As taxpayers, we're all paying the $18 billion or so a year that it takes to fund our prisons. Crime affects everyone, and The Inside Corporation has the potential to take a big "bite out of crime" by changing the lives of the people who commit crimes ... from the inside out.

The Rewards of Perseverance

There was a young photocopier salesman who, at five minutes to six o'clock on a Friday afternoon, after a solid week without a sale, decided to give up and find a new career. On his way out of the building he noticed a door he hadn't yet knocked on, and decided to give it one last try. The only person in that office that hadn't gone home was an older man who was at that moment cursing his copier for jamming. The man turned out to be the CEO, and the company had offices all over the country. That "final" sales call – the call that almost wasn't – resulted in over $100,000 in commissions in the first year alone.

I love that story. But I'm also haunted by it.

I love it because it says "Stick with it! Don't give up! The next sales call, the next formula, the next book, the next venture may be the one that sets you up for life, or at least gets you moving in the right direction."

I'm haunted by it because I realize how close *I* came to giving up when things were at their worst, and how many people actually *do* give up just one attempt short of the one that makes a lifetime of difference.

It illustrates one of the most important lessons I

think we can learn as human beings – that perseverance is vital to success; that you have to keep pounding on those doors – even when your knuckles are bleeding – until the right one opens. And it *will* open ... if you keep pounding.

I had come to a time in my life when a lot of different, wonderful doors were finally opening for me – doors that led to incredible opportunities and fulfillment. It was the domino effect of success, come to play fully in my life.

For example, the lease-purchase course was gaining widespread, mainstream acceptance. One indication of this was that it was approved by the Real Estate Commission of Georgia for continuing education credit for Realtors in Georgia. (It should soon be approved in other states around the country.)

Another strong indication of the program's acceptance was an invitation I received to teach the course to the sales agents in a New York real estate brokerage. In fact, one of the people I've trained to teach lease-purchasing has taught it to other realty companies since then. Given my history with the real estate sales industry and its rigid norms and conventions, I was pleasantly surprised to realize that some Realtors were actually beginning to open their minds to new ways of doing business.

Also, some speakers approached me who wanted to promote my lease-purchase course and The Mentor Group at local, regional, and national seminars and conventions. This was yet another sign that we were on the right track.

My personal trials and challenges, and the principles they have taught me – many of which are contained in this book and in the *Unlock!* course – also caught the public's attention. I began to get invitations asking me to tell my story to groups at various high school, grade schools, and civic clubs in the Atlanta area, such as the Rotary organization.

During this same period, we also worked out business arrangements with people all over the country whom we now call "Ambassadors." These people put us in touch with entities that have an interest in participating in the investment opportunities that The Mentor Group makes available.

We've even taken *Lease-Purchase Profits* and *Unlock!* to Mexico. As I mentioned earlier, Kelly and I fell in love with Mexico when we went down there on our honeymoon, and vowed that we'd go back. So we did go back – we went to Cancun, and fell even more in love with Mexico's Yucatan Peninsula. Unlike some places in Mexico, it's perfectly clean, almost everyone speaks English, and they have a 60-year master plan for development in the area, so they're taking their time and doing it right. They're trying to make the area the tourist capital of the world, and I think they're going to succeed. It's a paradise!

We got to know a lot of the people down there who are important in the Mexican real estate and tourist industries. Soon we began to have opportunities to do property transactions in the Yucatan, and to present the *Unlock!* program to hotel staffs in Cancun and the coastal area in the form of sales training programs. We've also taken groups of investors from the States to Cancun to introduce them to the tremendous investment opportunities that are there, and to give them seminars on the lease-purchase and *Unlock!* programs.

We now have strong connections in Cancun. In fact, Kelly and I have been able to go there *free* almost every month since our first visit. They pay our airfare, our food, and our hotel. When I say "they," I mean Oasis International, a resort/travel conglomerate – the largest in the area. They own Club America, a major travel wholesaler in the U.S.; they own their own charter planes; and they own the biggest resort in Cancun, plus a lot of land. They also have a resort in Puerto Aventuras that we've also been going to, which is a beautiful new beach resort development about an hour south of Cancun along the Caribbean coast.

Someday we'll go to Cancun just to play and lay in the sun. But we still have a lot we want to do there, so we spend most of our time teaching our courses, looking at investment opportunities, entertaining investors, networking, and meeting the right people.

Back on the home front, we launched a new phase of our business early in 1992: small group real estate consulting, or what we call "intensives." We started offering these because we realized that many people couldn't afford one-on-one consulting, yet still wanted my in-person, hands-on help, guidance, and motivation. So instead of consulting with just one person, we would take a half a dozen to a dozen people at one time, and I would do with them, as a group, what I would do with a single person in a one-on-one consulting setting.

The intensives quickly became very popular because they offered the added benefit of small group synergy. These individuals came together, and by the end of an intense weekend training program, they'd become a family of entrepreneurs with their own group energy. It was a tremendous advantage for them to be able to bond together with people who have the same interests. At first we would travel around the country to do the intensives, but eventually decided to have people come to us in Atlanta, where we have everything set up to do the course.

The Mentor Group, Inc. is all about mentoring. That's why I got into one-on-one consulting, and why we began offering the small group intensives for our programs. Sure, there are those people who can go through a workbook and tape course on their own and then go out and become successful at it without the personal guidance and motivation of an experienced mentor, but really, those people are few and far between. I would say that the vast majority of individuals need a hands-on mentor, or coach.

In mid-1992, we expanded our mentoring services beyond the one-on-one and small group consulting I had been offering for the lease-purchase program. We started a new and exciting aspect of The Mentor Group in which I help people establish what we call Independent Business Centers (IBCs), and get them up and running in their own businesses, rather than just training them to do deals here and there.

Helping someone create a successful Independent Business Center differs from my one-on-one consulting services in two important ways. First, instead of teaching them just the lease-purchase program, I teach them how to make money with several different business opportunities. Second, I'm more deeply involved with their businesses for a longer period of time on a personal basis.

The first business opportunity I teach the owner of an Independent Business Center is the lease-purchase program, because it's a great way to start generating income quickly, without having to invest a lot of up-front capital. The second opportunity is "precision" real estate investing: buying and selling the *right* properties. The third income producer I teach is the "IRA rollover." This basically involves using funds from self-directed IRA accounts to invest in new second mortgages that yield a much higher rate of return than what IRAs typically provide.

The fourth business opportunity I teach to the owners of Independent Business Centers is consulting. By that, I mean doing what I'm doing – consulting with people on lease-purchases, real estate investing, and IRA rollovers. These people act as associate consultants to people in their areas that can't afford to hire me. Of course, I make sure that they're well trained, knowledgeable, and experienced before they participate in this capacity, and then I start funneling consulting jobs through them.

The second way our Independent Business Center work differs from our one-on-one consulting services is in the depth and length of involvement I personally put into it. The whole point in working with Independent

Business Center clients is to go way beyond theory and guide them in a hands-on way to actually create a thriving business that can make them financially independent. This is more involved and has a wider scope than merely teaching them how to do lease-purchase deals. Getting a business off the ground and fine-tuning it so that it runs at maximum efficiency and profitability entails the full spectrum of business management operations, from marketing to setting up bookkeeping, from selecting the right location to getting the right people – in addition to the specific business opportunities we implement.

My relationship with these clients is ongoing and interactive. After the initial on-site work I do with them, I return to follow up with them periodically, or every few months as needed. In between, my staff and I answer their questions and make suggestions over the phone. I help them get their real estate licenses, if they need or want them. If they want to set up their own brokerages, I help them do that, and assist them in recruiting and selecting the sales staffs they need. I help find good independent contractors to work with. I help them create advertisements and marketing materials.

All of this revolves around the concept of mentoring. There are thousands and thousands of people out there trying to start businesses in real estate. They go to exciting seminars with hundreds of people, and buy hundreds and even thousands of dollars worth of books and tapes, but they never actually go out and do anything with that knowledge. Why? Because they go home and they don't have anybody to talk to, or to help them get going.

They need a mentor to guide them, to give them hands-on help – especially during the difficult formative phases of their enterprise. That's what we do. And that's what makes the difference. It's like having a real-life coach compared to reading a book. Would you rather learn karate by reading a book, or by taking private lessons from a black-belt instructor? There's something about the hands-on training, and knowing that there's someone there to help you that makes a real difference.

Mentoring is what we've always focused on in our one-on-one consulting, our small group intensives, and especially in our new Independent Business Center (IBC) program, which takes the mentoring process about as far as it can go. We try to always be there for our clients, to answer their questions when they call, and offer advice when they need help. That's why we don't work with more people than we can effectively handle. If we spread ourselves too thin, we can't give them the attention they need.

Nobody I know in our industry does one-on-one consulting the way we do – at least, nobody with our level of success. Almost everyone just sells books and tapes to make money for themselves. What we're interested in is establishing a relationship with people, so we can start funnelling business through them, and help them build successful companies.

When the hot days of summer rolled around that year – 1992 – I could no longer resist an urge that had been building up inside me for some time. Although I loved traveling around, consulting, and speaking, I had been feeling the need for quite awhile to get out and get my hands dirty, like I used to do when I'd buy and rehab properties. I had been keeping my eyes open for a good rehab property, and I found one that was perfect. It was on the north side of Atlanta, in Dunwoody.

We bought it and went to work. By "we" I mean our entire company. Everyone rolled up their sleeves and got involved. We took out six 40-yard dumpsters – that's 25 tons of trash! We ripped the walls out and rehabbed the whole building. We worked on it whenever our schedule allowed, burning the candle at both ends to get it done. It took three months, and when it was finished, I knew I had gotten the rehabbing bug out of my system, probably once and for all. As far as I'm concerned, it was the mother of all rehabs.

Not only did the Dunwoody project scratch an itch I had had for a long time, but it turned out to be an excellent investment for us. All in all, it was great therapy!

With all these good things flowing our way in business, something happened in the fall of that year that eclipsed even the most exciting of our entrepreneurial successes: my kids came "home." They say that if life is anything, it's interesting, and my life has certainly been no exception to that rule. In October, my ex-wife moved back to Atlanta with my children. It had been so devastating to me when she took them to Oregon during the lowest point in my life, that having them return to live just ten minutes away from where Kelly and I were living was a dream fulfilled.

We now get to see them all the time. We go bowling. We go camping. Every week or so, we have a special "date" with one of them. They'll sleep over with us and we'll do something fun that night.

We're also instilling in them the importance of the work ethic. We try to find little work projects that they can earn money doing, either in our business or at our home. We've opened saving accounts for each of them. If they put money in, we'll match it. This encourages them to save money rather than throw it away on video games and things like that. I suggest that they put at least half of the money they earn working for us in their savings accounts, but as it turns out, they've been socking almost all of it away into savings because we match whatever they put away dollar-for-dollar. It's great to see them exhibiting self control rather than just going out and blowing all their earnings on junk.

Well before my kids moved back to Atlanta, Kelly and I had moved into a luxury highrise residence, and purchased an office building for our company.

It was okay living in one bedroom of a house that was our office for awhile – especially while we needed to put every penny back into our business, and while we were spending *all* our time on the road and working. We were like Einstein and Edison and those kind of guys who were so engrossed in what they were doing that they slept where they worked. But one day we woke up and said, "Hey, we don't have to do this anymore. We're making money, the business is on a solid foundation, and we've got great people working with us. Why don't we get a real place to live away from work?" So we did. And luckily we chose a place that was big enough for my children, too.

My Guardian Angel

I have a guardian angel. Strange as that may sound, it's true. For years he has watched over me, protected me, guided me, helped me make the right decisions, and steered me around what could have been disasters on many different occasions.

My guardian angel's name is Bill – Bill Taaffe. He's about six feet tall, slender, and is currently in his late 40s, though he looks a lot younger.

You've probably figured out by now that Bill is not a real guardian angel ... at least not in the technical sense. By that, I mean he has a real body that sweats and bleeds and can't walk through walls. But as far as I'm concerned, he qualifies as a *bona fide* guardian angel in every other way.

I met Bill when I first came to Atlanta. He had been with Balcor, a huge real estate development and investment company that was sold to American Express for over $100 million. For about the first two years that Bill worked with me, he didn't take a dime in compensation. He worked for free. He did that, he says, because he was looking for another "rocket ship." He had helped grow Balcor from a one-room operation to a mega-corporation, and he saw that same kind of potential in me and what I was trying to do.

When I asked Bill to work with me full-time, he had me read Stephen R. Covey's book, *The Seven Habits of Highly Effective People,* and then wanted to discuss my feelings about it. The book addresses many of the moral and ethical principles that support people and businesses that are truly successful, and Bill wanted to be sure that I agreed with those concepts before he committed to invest his life with me. In the siding business, I had been taught to say whatever it took to make the sale (which is the reason I got out of it). Bill wanted to be sure and to feel comfortable about my ethics now, both as a person and as a businessman, before he committed to come on board with me.

You see, everything about Bill is based on integrity, character, and moral fiber. He's like an anchor. He's constant and stable. He's always positive. He's the most spiritual person I've ever met. Nothing shakes him up. If something major happens – like a disaster – he freezes time and stops and thinks about it. He acts, he doesn't *re*act. He's a person with vision – with "seven-figure thinking."

Yet he doesn't want anything faster than we deserve it, and he's not willing to go into the gray area to get it. He's very conservative, so consequently we're a very stable company. We save money. We're not into opulence. We don't do anything just for show. Everybody who meets him is automatically more comfortable with me because of him.

Here's an illustration of how Bill does things, and how he has influenced me. Early in our relationship, we would be working on a marketing piece, and I'd write something up and take it in to show him. He'd read it and say, "What is it you're trying to say here?" I would tell him, and he'd say, "Well, that's not what you're saying," or "This may be misleading to some people." Because Bill was so adamant about staying away from any gray areas, he would tell me to go back and work on it.

So I'd go work on it, then come back in and show it to him again. He'd read it again, then look up at me, and I'd laugh because I'd know that I still had some gray stuff in there. I'd go back and work on it some more, then take it back to Bill. But this time, I wouldn't even sit down – I'd just look at him and turn around and go back and fix it.

This "training" process went on for a period of months. I got to the point that I'd be taking something I'd written to his office for him to read, but before I even got to his door, I'd turn around and go back and work on it. Then I'd stand up at my desk and sit back down again, and finally I wouldn't even get up. Now I'm at the point where I don't have to go through this process. Bill has been very successful in being a mentor to me, and teaching me his thinking and perspectives.

It's like he's now inside me. And yet we're perfect opposites in terms of personality and who we are as individuals. We're the perfect match – like the left hand and the right hand.

To Bill, character is a far more valuable commodity than money. As far as he's concerned, if someone makes a billion dollars the wrong way, it's not worth it. He believes that if you live your life right and you do things the way you're supposed to do them, the energy of the world works *for* you – it comes together and makes things happen.

That's exactly what has happened to The Mentor Group. We went from zero to $50,000 a year, to $500,000 a year, and from the way things are going we'll probably continue to grow and prosper exponentially throughout the years ahead. It's amazing how things work.

Bill is like the father I never had, the best friend I never had, and the ideal mentor. He was the one who really helped me get The Mentor Group off the ground. It was his belief in me and loyalty to me, plus his incredible talents, energy, trustworthiness, and stabilizing influence that did it. From the beginning, he has taken care of all the finances, the accounting, the checks, the legal matters, and just about every other management and support function that has kept the company going strong and growing larger.

Bill's official title in The Mentor Group, Inc. is "General Manager." But that's only because "Guardian Angel" would look funny on a business card.

Dreams

I've never been short of dreams. Even when my life was at its lowest ebb, my hopes and goals for the future helped keep me going. I love turning dreams into realities. You could say it's my favorite hobby. And why not? When you really think about it, making a dream come true is an act of creation. You're taking something out of your heart and putting it out there in the material world – making it a real thing ... something that you can touch or feel inside.

In the past few years, many of my most cherished dreams have come true – like finding the perfect wife, and building a successful, stable, rewarding business.

Several others are now in the process of coming true. For instance, I've wanted to get into consulting with top national corporations for some time now. Recently, we've taken the time and made the effort to make that begin to happen. Although we're just out of the gate with this aspect of our business, we've already had some very positive experiences with top-notch clients, including American Express, Lego, and Lanier Worldwide.

Our corporate consulting work falls into two primary niches, or areas of focus. One is the supervised employee, which is the entry-level type of employee. Business owners and managers typically don't invest training dollars in these types of workers because they don't believe it will make a substantial difference to their revenues or profits.

They couldn't be more wrong. These supervised employees make their companies what they are. They need a lot of positive reinforcement because they're usually the ones that are identified and stereotyped as being the least valuable. The *Unlock!* principles, coupled with the positive perspectives we teach that focus on their particular situations, have and will continue to improve the lives and the productivity of these employee groups.

The other niche we're hitting in our corporate consulting work focuses on helping management respond positively to a general trend that can be seen in every corner of corporate America today. Many of the big corporations have had their heydays, and are now suffering all kinds of problems. They're taking losses and having to lay off people and generally downsize. They're realizing that there's a lot of waste and inefficiency within companies today, as there has been over the past decade. They're realizing that they need to cut back, tighten up, and work more as independent entrepreneurial departments.

In his book, *Liberation Management*, Tom Peters says many things that really make sense: "In today's environment," he writes, "the essence of strategy is not the structure of a company's products and markets, but the dynamics of its behavior.... I always tell our people to think small, think start-up, think how you'd do it if you were working in a garage."

Peters also makes a strong point for breaking out of the mold. He talks about "putting zanies in charge," and claims, "If you don't feel crazy, you are not in touch with the times." He says big companies need to bring in someone from outside their own businesses, or perhaps from outside their industries altogether, who is crazy, zany, and bonkers – who can stir things up, cut through all the baloney and show what needs to be done and what *can* be done. This is important because people too often become routinized in their corporate cultures. In a way, they fall asleep. They need to be jolted. They need to be awakened to new possibilities, and to new, creative ways of thinking.

That's exactly what we, The Mentor Group, now do for corporations. And we plan to do it more and more as time goes on. It's one of our long-term programs.

We also have other dreams that are waiting for us to make them real. After all, what's a future if you don't have dreams to pull you into it?

These dreams are in various stages of development. One is almost complete – just a few months away from the final stage of realization. For a long time, we've wanted to write a consumer-oriented book about lease-purchasing and have it published by a national publishing house. If everything proceeds as planned, this dream will very soon become a reality. We've written it, and it's now in the hands of a national publishing company, and is due out in June of 1993.

The book is called *Lease-Purchase, America!* We

hope it will wake the general population up to the alternative and the opportunities of lease-purchasing real estate. After all, it's not a new concept. People have been doing it for years to get cars, for instance, whether they call it lease-purchase, lease-to-own, or rent-to-own. Eighty-five percent of Infinity's car sales are lease-to-own transactions. Any newspaper's car sales section is going to be filled with lease offers. Everything these days is lease, lease, lease.

That's the exact same thing as our lease-purchase program, except that we're dealing with houses rather than cars. Our book will help people to realize and understand that they've known about lease-purchasing already for years, but they've just been calling it something else.

Lease-Purchase, America! will be the first book ever to be published about lease-purchasing, and it is directed to the average consumer.

One of our dreams that is currently on the drawing board is to produce two infomercials for national exposure. One will promote our lease-purchase program, the other will introduce the world to *Unlock!*

Also, we have a goal to expand our training efforts geographically. One of our associates is from Australia. We're planning to do some work over there, and after that, in some other foreign countries.

Dreams are wound up tightly with desires. All my life I've had the desire to help people. This has given me the motivation and energy to do everything good I've ever done in my business life. Today, it is shifting the focus of our business from teaching people how to make money in real estate to helping them unlock their own potential for true success and lasting happiness.

Sure, we'll continue to help people generate wealth through lease-purchasing and other techniques. But I know that if people's attitudes aren't sound, and their heads aren't on straight, all the wealth in this world won't make them happy. When you really think about it, it's an interesting relationship. Money won't make you happy. But if you don't have any, it can make you very unhappy. In mathematical terms: money doesn't equal happiness; yet happiness rarely exists if money isn't part of the equation.

So our emphasis is currently shifting toward the full-time teaching of the human development principles found in the *Unlock!* program. This will give people the solid foundation on which they can build their financial houses with the bricks and sticks of our money-making programs. Soon, part of our thrust will also address interpersonal relationships. We're planning programs for families, kids, couples, and relationships in general, both business and personal.

One of the reasons why we're setting up the Independent Business Centers – the IBCs – is so that those centers can handle a lot of the business that's out there, and let us concentrate more on personal development programs for people in every walk of life – whether they're CEOs of Fortune 500 companies or inmates in our country's prisons. That's what has made the biggest change in my own life, and that's what I feel I should do. Teaching these types of programs is also what I really enjoy doing most.

When people ask what Kelly and I do when we're not working, they get a fairly short and simple answer, because we're almost always working. And we're always working together. I don't know of *any* other couple that spends as much time together as we spend. Aside from doing things with the kids, going to church, exercising, reading, and taking in a few movies, there really aren't any pastimes that take any significant amount of our time.

Sure, we take time away from our work. We try to stay balanced. We just don't take the time everybody else takes. But then, we're trying to do things that most people aren't trying to do. Our work is our hobby. We love it. We're building our dreams together. And we're building something good and lasting.

When I have the time to kick back and think about where my life's path has taken me in the last few years, as compared to where I have been, I feel extremely blessed. Like Job of the Bible story, everything that has been taken away from me has been or is being restored. And in most cases, what is coming back to me is better, stronger, and more significant and lasting than what I had before.

I also feel blessed that my rags-to-riches-to-rags-to-riches story is giving people hope and motivating them to hang in there and keep working to rise above whatever ruts they fall into. I remember finding out that Walt Disney, like many of the business greats of our time, went bankrupt several times before he created his financial empire. This made me realize that setbacks don't have to be permanent. I can't begin to describe what it means to me to hear that people around the country are now reading my life story and coming away with a similar "I can bounce back" attitude.

All in all, my life is definitely on the upswing. And after all the hard lessons I've learned, I have a feeling that my roller coaster ride has finally stopped. God willing, hand in hand with Kelly, I will continue to climb steadily upward.

A Positive Attitude: The Amazing Grace

Attitude is a popular word these days. Everywhere you go, you hear statements like, "Boy, does he have an attitude!" or "Get an attitude!" All the problems that have come my way have taught me a valuable lesson that makes the suffering I've gone through worthwhile. It's a lesson about attitude.

The word *attitude* can denote something positive or something negative. That's because attitudes themselves are either positive or negative. They are not fence-sitters.

Attitude has become a very popular word because we are beginning to realize what an incredibly important role our attitudes play in shaping our lives. We are beginning to understand that good things and bad things happen to everyone, and that it's not *what* happens to us, but *how* we perceive and respond toward what is happening to us that makes us happy or sad, relaxed or nervous, hopeful or fearful.

And that's what attitude is: the perception of and response to what goes on in our lives.

On a very simple level, it's like the old story about

the half-full/half-empty glass of water. Two people are given a glass of water. Both of their glasses have been filled to the halfway mark. The first person sees a glass of water that is half empty. He begins to complain. He feels victimized that he was robbed of the other half portion of water. He makes himself a "loser." After drinking, he is empty, bitter, and thirsty. The second person looks and sees a glass that is half full. He rejoices that he has been given half a glass of water where before he had nothing. He gives thanks, and feels that the world is a loving, caring place, and that he is a winner. When he drinks, he is happy and his thirst is quenched.

There is only one difference between these two men: attitude. Treated equally, one makes himself an embittered loser whose negative energy will attract negative things, while the other becomes a positive, happy winner whose "good vibrations" will bring positive people and opportunities his way.

I'm now going to give you a concept that is absolutely, monumentally important. Here it is: *No matter what happens to you, you can find some positive way to look at it. And how you look at it will directly affect your level of happiness, and even your future.*

Do you follow me? Do you understand the importance of that powerful concept? Simply stated, I'm saying that *you* are in command of your own happiness. Other people and external objects and events that you can't always control do not ultimately dictate how happy you are. *You* do!

It all comes down to your attitude about what's

happening to you.

Believe me, I know. I had more setbacks, heart-breaks, and outright disasters in the space of just a few years than the vast majority of people will have in their lifetimes. I could easily have taken refuge in drugs, alcohol, crime, depression, bitter apathy, violent anger, or even suicide.

Why didn't I? Because my faith in God, in myself, and in tomorrow enabled me to adjust my perspective of what was happening to me. I was able to say, "There *is* something positive about this. There *is* a reason for this."

For instance, if I hadn't lost my business in New York, I would have had to spend a lot of time flying back and forth between Rochester and Atlanta. And because I was not there to oversee things, maybe some-one would have done something wrong and I would have been penalized, or worse. Or, more likely, maybe I would have continued in that business for the rest of my life, and things would have gone fine. If so, I would never have learned the lessons that my challenges and suffering have taught me. I would never have written this book. I would never have had the chance to help people get through their problems. In short, I would never have fulfilled my full potential or my mission in life.

If I had never had the experience of being arrested and spending time in jail, I would not have the empathy for inmates I now have; I would not have extended myself to help them rise above their circumstances; and I would never have created The Inside Corporation.

Nor would I have learned how to be patient and to accept things that can't be changed; how to relax, think, and meditate. I wouldn't have learned that we are lucky if we have even one *true* friend, and that such a friend deserves all our love and appreciation.

If I had not lost my credit and cash, I would never have developed my creativity. Without these things, I was able to not only survive but prosper. I was able to create a solid, successful new business, staffed by some of the best, most capable people I have ever met. Not having credit has made me humble. This has helped make it possible for me to rise to the top again.

If I had never had to start over again, with absolutely nothing but what was inside me, I would not have the quiet confidence in myself I have today. I realize now that I was lucky the first time I "made" it. It was easy. But "easy" is not what I want now. I want solid stability, longevity – something that will last for the rest of my life and hopefully beyond, in the lives of the people I have had the opportunity to touch.

If I had not "lost" my unfulfilling marriage, I would never have found the rewarding, joyful, mature marital relationship I now enjoy.

But what if you can't find a positive perspective about something that has happened? For instance, what was positive about both of my parents dying at the relatively young age of 58? In cases like this, I think you have to have faith that there is some purpose – some ultimately good or merciful design – in what happens. My parents, for example, passed on to the next life fairly quickly. They could have suffered through years of pain and fear before finally dying, as so many people do. So who am I to say that their early deaths weren't blessings in disguise? I choose to believe that their passings were, in fact, blessings.

It was a little more difficult to find anything positive in the fact that I lived thousands of miles away from my four children for so long. Nothing could ever fill up the hole their absence made in my life. But even before they moved back to Atlanta, I was able to make an attitude adjustment that turned what had been a nearly unbearable sorrow into something more positive.

You see, during that time I was able to take comfort in the fact that they knew that they had a Dad who really, really, wanted them, and loved them, and worried about them, and wanted the best for them. At the same time, they had a wonderful mother. Now that they're back in Atlanta, they have the same loving mother and father – but now their father is right around the corner. And they're at a time in their lives when they really need my support and the guidance I can give them.

The ongoing challenge is to maintain a positive perspective and attitude when things go bad, when life gets tough. I am acutely aware of the fact that my only link to sanity, happiness, and success is my good attitude. Without it I would drown.

For that reason, I'm very careful to protect and nurture my positive mindset. I stay away from anyone or anything that will dump negative, evil, or depressing thoughts into my mind. Horror movies are a prime example. I simply can't watch them. I will not tolerate that kind of evil, satanical abuse.

I can't stand to be around negative people for the same reason. I've developed something like an allergic reaction to them. On many occasions, I've been with people when the talk turns negative. I get out of there immediately. After all I've been through, I literally cannot endure it.

Being positive is like anything else – it gets easier with practice. But until you come to the point where you're a "master" at it, you have to constantly struggle to keep a good attitude.

I speak from experience. I have gone through times that were so bad that I lost my positive edge. During those periods I felt like I didn't want to go on living. I even thought of becoming a cop and putting an end to it all by getting shot.

But somehow, every time, my faith helped me pull myself up out of despair, regain my positive attitude, and get on with the task of living.

Now, living is a joy – not a task.

That's my message and my challenge. No matter how bad things get, no matter how black life appears, you have to hang on and look deep within yourself to find that kernel of positive, joyous, confident happiness that is within us all. It may be tiny. It may be encrusted with years of negative input and experience. But it's there.

Once you find it, hang onto it. Feed it day and night with positive thoughts. Avoid negative influences. As you do, it will grow and become a powerful force that will literally transform your life.

I'm reminded of the famous early American hymn,

Amazing Grace. Listen to the words ...

> *Amazing grace! How sweet the sound*
> *That saved a wretch like me.*
> *I once was lost, but now am found,*
> *Was blind, but now I see.*
>
> *Through many dangers, toils, and snares,*
> *I have already come;*
> *'Tis grace hath brought me safe thus far,*
> *And grace will lead me home.*

The amazing "grace" that is the natural result of a positive attitude has led me from the jail cell to the speaker's podium; from the rags of bankruptcy court to the riches of a prosperous business; from an unhappy marriage to one that is filled with love and understanding.

As the song says, it has brought me safe thus far. And it will lead me home.

It can do the same for you.

What People Are Saying About John Ross and the *Unlock!* Program

"I am most impressed with your program and with your willingness to share your experiences with those who can most benefit from them.... It appears you have taken the most appropriate step in designing a program aimed at turning lives around: to focus on practical and realizable goals." – S.N., United States Senator

"For the first time in a long time I feel I am in control of my destiny.... I want to thank John Ross for being a true mentor to me in my life." – B.S., gemologist

"It is difficult for me to put into words how much your time has meant to me both financially and on a personal level." – S.G., businessperson

"You and your family of mentors are incredible. You open up your arms and share all of your love, care, and support. Your program "*Unlock!*" is dynamite because it helps one discover and unleash the wealth of resources that are hidden in all of us." – G.F., businessperson

"John Ross gives you something to take home and apply to almost every aspect of life." – J.R.W., political organization leader

"I can't say 'thank you' enough for showing me the way to a better future, not only for myself, but for my entire family." – D.N., businessperson

"It's wonderful to feel so alive. Your are an incredible influence on me. Thank you!" – G.F., businessperson

"A blaze has to start with a spark, and I want to thank you for igniting a spark in me.... You have given me an avenue for my dreams to come true." – P.H., businessperson

"Your proven business savvy, enthusiasm, and motivation touches all." – C.C., president, national business organization

"Anyone can practice the information you teach and grow from it personally and financially. The time I spent with you was probably the most valuable time I've spent as long as I can remember." – G.G., businessperson

"John's presence is so unforgettable.... John is the uncommon man for common folks." – K.B., corporate president

"John's inspiration has been a marvelous blessing in my life." – T.M., real estate investor

"John has given me many different visions, which challenge me to take steps to explore a higher goal in life." – J.H., businessperson

"What a great experience to work one-on-one with John. It is so much easier to grow when you're not fighting your fears.... Thank you John. What a positive experience!" – J.S., businessperson

"Thanks for all your help, advice, and encouragement. I now believe I will succeed." – J.C., businessperson

"Your experience and knowledge will help guide many of us as we make decisions that will affect the rest of our lives." – M.C., president, youth business organization

John Ross' Lease-Purchase Program
Wins Raves Reviews

"With your creative lease-purchase techniques, I am well on my way to earning a six-figure income and becoming financially independent.... In the last couple months, I have consistently set up one to two transactions per week for cash profit, and virtually no money down. In a world of real estate get-rich quick schemes and other false-hope business opportunities, you provide something that is practical, real, and *solid*." – S.G., Realtor/investor

"John, your great program is working for me. On my first venture, the buyer and the seller (a doctor) were so happy about how quick and easy it went, they each gave me more business! This first deal made me $500 an hour. Not bad." – J.P., investor

"John, your lease-purchase concept ... has given us, as owners, and our staff, the nuts and bolts required to proceed in our business. Your book is straightforward yet comprehensive. We've already had success with it, and can see our way clear to doing a great deal more." – D.Y., real estate agency broker/owner

"This lease-purchase concept is the best way I've seen for an individual to be involved with properties and make real cash today. Whether you're a Realtor or an investor, lease-purchase is *the* way of the '90s." – C.R., award-winning Realtor

"Within just one month I've been able to put together two lease-purchase deals amounting to over $3,000 in cash profits in my pocket with only a few hours work a week." – M.J., president, financial consulting firm

"We worked with John's lease-purchase techniques and within a week found our ideal home and moved in! Lease-purchase helped us to make a move quick." – J.E., homeowners

"Thank you so much. I've had so many inquiries about your book and your availability to lecture on your lease-purchase concept. We want you to come back for another show and talk more about lease-purchase. Our audience is thirsting for this information." – J.G., radio talk show executive

"I never thought I could own a home, and without lease-purchase, I'd still be renting. The unique opportunity of lease-purchase has allowed me to own a home with monthly payments equivalent to renting. Now I've got all the benefits of home ownership, and my money is working for me." – C.M., psychologist

"As individuals in the ever-changing real estate industry, our knowledge is never complete. Your information is very useful, and your ideas have brought new life to the industry." – L.M., chairman, real estate agent organization

"During the '80s I made a lot of money by wheeling and dealing in real estate. Unfortunately, the crash came. After reading about your concepts, it revitalized my ambitions to succeed. I thank you for going public with your lease-purchase ideas." – R.Q., Realtor

"This is an idea that is revolutionizing the real estate market throughout the country." – national real estate leadership organization

"Your program, by far, is the most realistic for today's economy." – L.L., businessperson/investor

"You *must* read and hear John Ross. John has shown us the way by using the lease-purchase alternative. People with no cash or credit are able to purchase real estate. If you want to sell your real estate, you can broaden the number of people who would like to purchase your home. If you are in the market to buy real estate, this program is for you." – S.B., real estate investor organization president

"As a group president and major investor, I've been wondering if there were any new ideas on how to buy and sell real estate. I was very impressed with your techniques. I completed my first deal within one week... You have created a lot of excitement with the easy techniques of your system. Thanks again ..." – M.G., real estate group president/investor

"Your knowledge in real estate is exceptional. The material you've provided in your lease-purchase book is easy to understand. The information seemed to be tailored specifically to my needs and the current market.... I thank God for this opportunity." – G.G., businessperson

"Before getting involved, I'd heard lots of interesting and favorable comments about your lease-purchase system. Thank you for sharing your secrets and knowledge with the rest of us in the world." – S.R., founder, real estate investors organization

"We read your materials, listened to your tapes, and had you work with us one-on-one. That investment of time and money has rewarded us with $35,000.00 in just a few months." – L.G., real estate company associate broker

"Thank you, John Ross, for your training in lease-purchase.... A dream come true. *Viva* John Ross!" – P.L., Realtor

John Ross and The *Inside Corporation* Applauded From All Sides

"I applaud you for the work that you're doing to help our inmate population, and I hope you continue to involve us with your progress and results." – N.G., United States Congressman

"Being a 21 year old male with nine more years to do, I want to thank you for giving me another path to follow when I get out of jail ... even from here I am using your teachings to help my family on the street. I thank you and my family thanks you." – L.H., inmate

"In my life, I've tasted success. But through a series of events it has all fallen apart. I had lost a very important part of myself: the ability to dream. The negative prison environment only added to my depression. Yes, I've made mistakes, but I now can learn from them and move forward. All this and more is what your classes gave me. They have once again awakened my desire to dream." – D.E.R., inmate.

"Thank you for sharing your information to better the future of inmates. I hope that this program will truly make a difference in the lives of those served." – P.H., state lieutenant governor

"I want to thank you for you efforts in coming into prisons.... We need help from the outside – people who will be willing to see us for what we really are and to see our potential." – R.G., inmate

"Your message is just what I needed to hear." – P.K., inmate

"The Lord must have sent you to us.... Your sessions have provided me and others the insight to enable us to make a better way of making money ... Mr. Ross, I hope you and your wife will come back every week. The inmates have a great need for someone like yourself that will help them prepare for re-entry back into society." – O.V., inmate

"Bring him back ... we can learn from him." – J.G., inmate

"Money is always easier to donate than time. You gave of your time and self.... I am truly grateful that I was afforded the opportunity to meet and learn from you." – L.T., inmate

"This seminar has really begun to give me vision.... I really and truly believe that this program will be very beneficial to hundreds or maybe thousands of guys who need encouragement and motivation to do positive things upon release from prison." – L.P., inmate

"I will be going home soon, and I need all the help I can get. I think this program will help me not come back to prison. I would like to thank Mr. Ross for caring." – T.W.F., inmate

"You have a very innovative and thoughtful program of education. Teaching the values of private enterprise to inmates of correctional institutions is certainly deserving of recognition." – M.M., U.S. Chamber of Commerce official

"We inmates are often the forgotten ones – the dregs of society that no one cares about. You, who have come to us with 'the winds of change,' have given us something to believe in: ourselves!" – M.D., inmate

"Thanks for not showing me how to just survive, but more importantly, for showing me how to succeed." – M.H., inmate

"I'm not too good at writing. I just want you to know that I do appreciate you coming out to teach us." – V.C., inmate

"Your program in the prisons, with focus on personal self-worth and self-esteem, appear to be right on target to help prisoners plan for a new beginning with their lives 'on the outside.'" – T.P., state senator

"I am a parole violator. Maybe if the system would have had workshops like yours before, I might not have returned to prison." – E.B., inmate

"You are a very positive person and that in itself has made me feel like 'I can do it' when I get out. Most of the guys in here have never believed in themselves. You are just what we need." – F.P., inmate

"I really enjoyed the talk by Mr. Ross ... programs of this type are just the shot in the arm that some of us need ... not only to hold our heads up high once again, but to help develop an attitude that will assure we make this our last trip to prison." – C.M., inmate

"Many [inmates] seem to be lost in a kind of vain hopelessness. Mr. Ross' workshops may be the fix these prisoners need." – M.G.S., inmate

"By teaching the mechanics of money-making to this particular group, [John] might permanently alter the paths some of our lives have taken and thereby benefit society as a whole." – L.M., inmate

Dear Friend,

I hope you enjoyed reading about my life. Fortunately for me, I have been blessed to meet and work with some exceptional mentors. In working side-by-side with them, I have learned things that have never been put into writing - things that can only be learned through the dynamics of one-on-one mentoring. (Thus, the name of the company: The Mentor Group.)

I've learned principles of lifetime significance, such as the value of long-term thinking, the value of mutually beneficial relationships, and the importance of integrity, character and genuineness. I use these principles *every day* in my business and personal life.

I now spend much of my time teaching and mentoring individuals, speaking to groups & organizations, and conducting corporate training in the United States and abroad. If you enjoyed the book, or if you know of a company or a friend that could benefit from my services please write and let me know.

My phone in Atlanta is 404-936-8060, or write 4279 Roswell Road, Suite 102-320, Atlanta, Georgia 30342. Thank you.

Always believe in yourself,

John J. Ross